In the Ward

Lawren Harris, Toronto & the Idea of North

Andrew Hunter

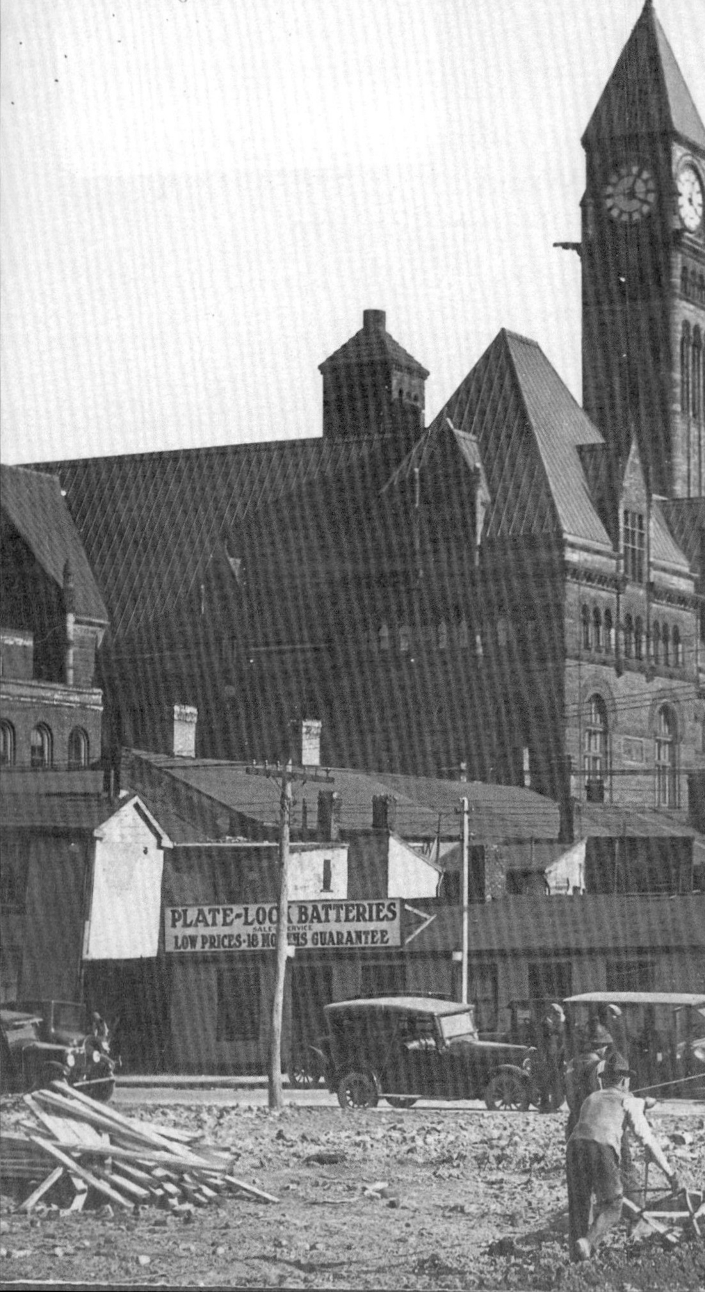
PLATE-LOC BATTERIES
LOW PRICES-18 MO GUARANTEE

I've been acquainted for such a long time with ambivalence—that's why I'm here, up this river in Canada, myself alone... I'm going north toward or into (I hope) a specificity, a few patches of ground, a vista, a now as well as a then.

— C.S. GISCOMBE, *INTO AND OUT OF DISLOCATION* (2000)[i]

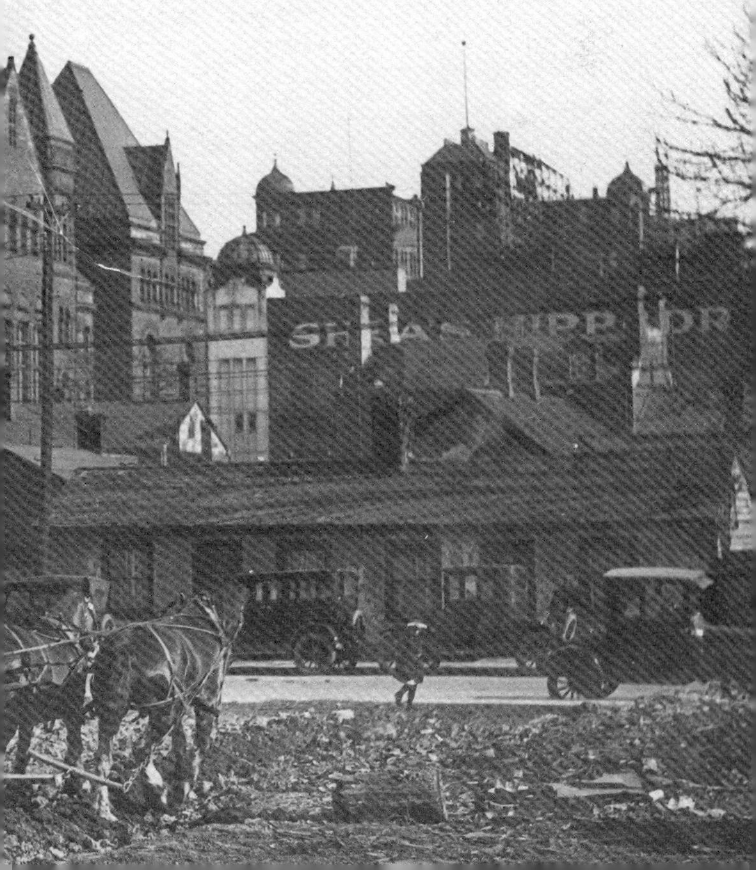

Front cover: Lawren S. Harris, Detail of *In the Ward* (1920), oil on canvas
Inner cover: Unknown photographer, Walton Street, East of Elizabeth (1975)

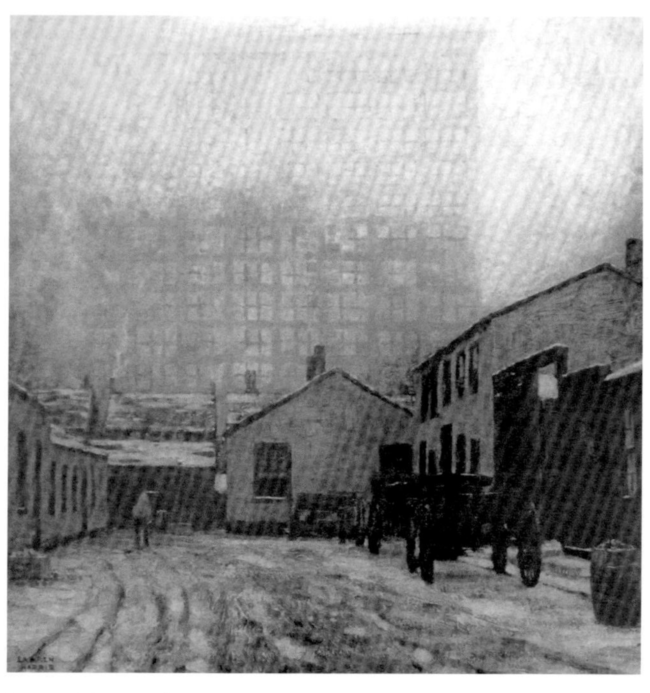

Lawren S. Harris, *The Eaton Manufacturing Building* (1911), oil on canvas

Pages 2–3: Unknown photographer, Plowing the ground for Eaton's Parking Lot at James and Louisa Streets, looking southwest to the Old City Hall (1925)

We are at the AGO in downtown Toronto on Dundas Street West, looking at Lawren Harris's Lake Superior canvas, an austere scene of dark islands and sheets of raking light cutting through sparse clouds. "It really looks like that," I tell my daughter Claire. "I think many people here in Toronto assume otherwise, that it's pure fantasy, but it's quite real, the light really does come down in sheets like that." We are visiting the exhibition *The Idea of North: The Paintings of Lawren Harris*. Claire scans the walls, moving back in time from the 1930s to the early 1920s, to the Arctic, Rocky Mountains, Lake Superior—iconic views that have become imbedded deeply, through concerted effort, in many people's idea of Canada. "Of course, I can't say that for all his images," and then I quote Glenn Gould, from *The Idea of North*, (1967):

Like all but very few Canadians, I've had no real experience of the North—I've remained, of necessity, an outsider. And the North has remained, for me a convenient place to dream about, spin tall tales about and, in the end, avoid.[ii]

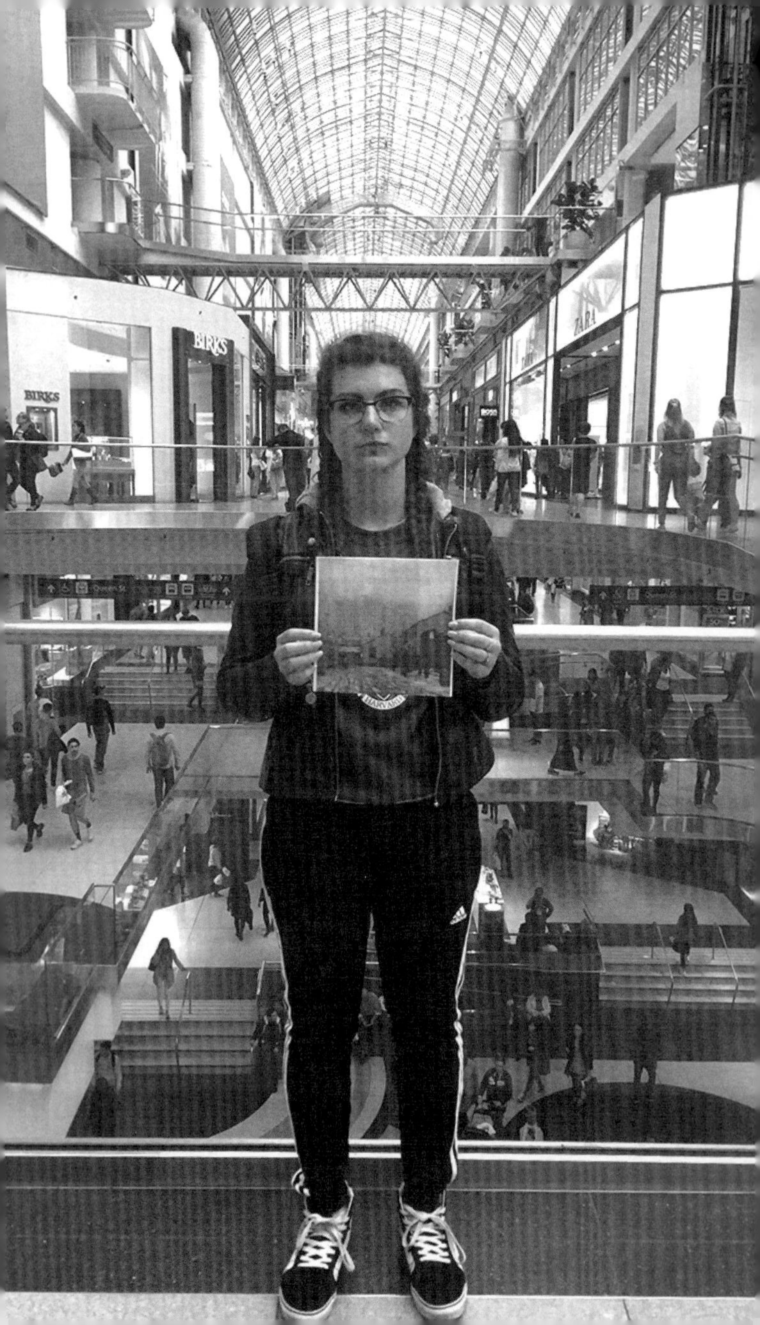
BIRKS
BIRKS
ZARA

Outsiders, dreamers, tall tales. "Harris's visionary North, his idea of North, was really shaped here, in Toronto," I explain, "It is a view from here, constructed in and informed by this place, and Harris's ideas will in turn shape this place." I hand her a picture of a painting, *The Eaton Manufacturing Building* (1911) (*see page 6*). Another time, another way of seeing. Harris in the belly of a dense urban scene, the building rests, bathed in a distinctly different light than illuminates his Lake Superior work. A warm morning haze glows above a shadowed courtyard. "Harris started here," I tell her, "and that's where we need to start too, because there is a backstory to the exhibition, a story I have contemplated and constructed while the exhibition toured Los Angeles and Boston, places where we focused on positioning Harris within an established history of painting in the Americas, along with Arthur Dove, Marsden Hartley and Georgia O'Keeffe. But here, back in Toronto, we need to understand his roots, roots that will point to Toronto's future, build a prologue that will become the epilogue."

And so we exit and head east on Dundas toward Yonge, into the traces of the Ward, a convenient place to dream about, spin tall tales about and in the end...

Left: Claire and Andrew Hunter, Site of Lawren S. Harris's The Eaton Manufacturing Building at north end of Eaton Centre (2016)

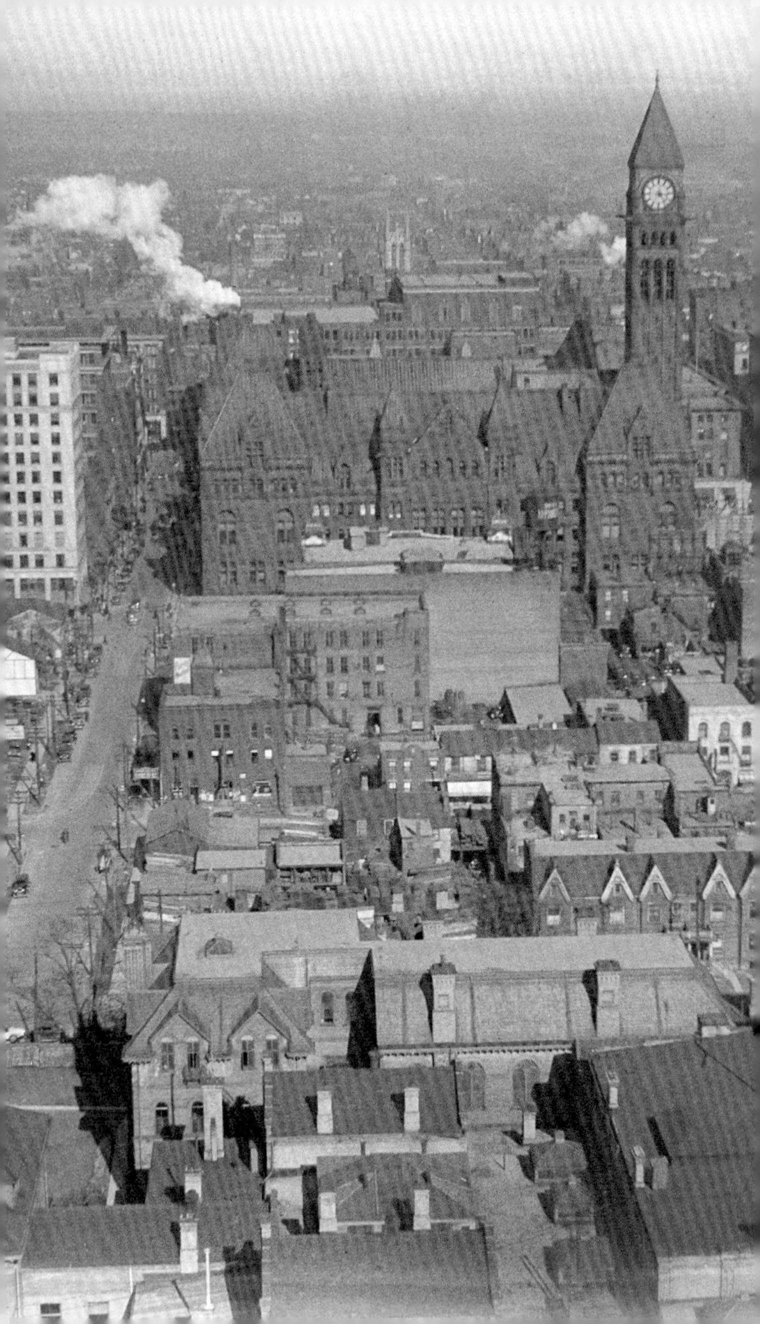

Part 1
In St. John's Ward

Morning...

Bathed in the morning sun I walk up street
Through the crowds swarming to the daily grind.
The air is fresh and cool.
Everyone is alert and ready for the day's grind.
People are friendly and smile, and give how-d' you-do's
and how-are-you's so easily.
They enjoy their fellows and the lilt of the morning.
The rattle and clanging of streetcars, the roar of
heavily laden trucks, the piercing bleat of arrogant
motor horns—all discordant noises of
the street
Bespeak to them the romantic import of human affairs.
Facing the morning sun people swarm to the daily grind...

— LAWREN HARRIS, FROM *MORNING AND EVENING* (1922) [iii]

Left: William James, View of the Ward looking east from the roof of the Canada Life Building (1910)

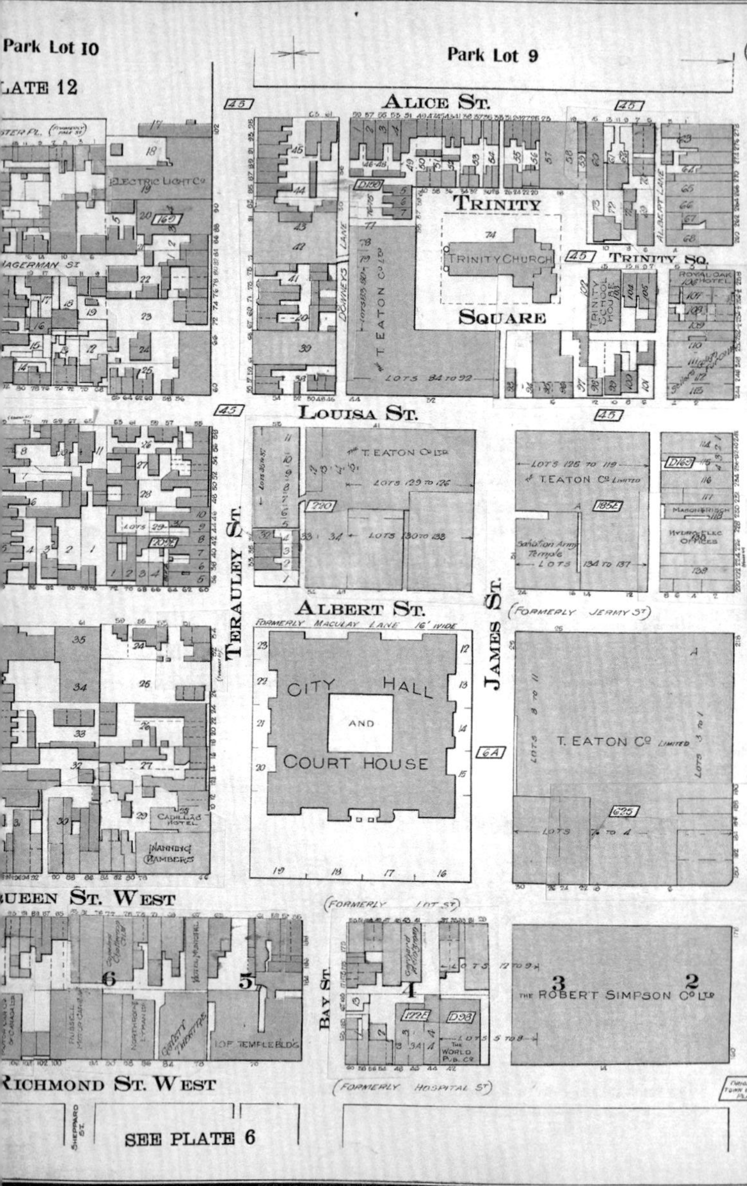

Park Lot 10
PLATE 12
Park Lot 9
ALICE ST.
ELECTRIC LIGHT Co
HAGERMAN ST
TRINITY
TRINITY CHURCH
TRINITY SQ.
SQUARE
T. EATON Co LTD
DOWNEYS LANE
TRINITY SCHOOL HOUSE
ROYAL OAK HOTEL
ALBERT LANE
LOTS 84 TO 92
LOUISA ST.
T. EATON Co LTD
LOTS 129 TO 126
LOTS 130 TO 133
LOTS 125 TO 119
T. EATON Co LIMITED
Salvation Army Temple
LOTS 134 TO 137
MASON & RISCH
HYDRO-ELEC OFFICES
TERAULEY ST.
ALBERT ST.
FORMERLY MACULAY LANE 16' WIDE
JAMES ST.
(FORMERLY JERMY ST)
CITY HALL
AND
COURT HOUSE
T. EATON Co LIMITED
LOTS 8 TO 11
LOTS 3 TO 1
LOTS 7 TO 4
CADILLAC HOTEL
MANNING CHAMBERS
QUEEN ST. WEST
(FORMERLY LOT ST)
GAIETY THEATRE
I.O.F. TEMPLE BLDG
BAY ST.
LOTS 12 TO 9
THE WORLD PUB. Co
LOTS 5 TO 8
THE ROBERT SIMPSON Co LTD
RICHMOND ST. WEST
(FORMERLY HOSPITAL ST)
SHEPPARD ST.
SEE PLATE 6

All these lives pivot around the solid presence of your architecture —static bodies, standing rigid, as if called for inspection, seemingly posed, towered-over and dwarfed by your massive weight of red brick, squared timber, quarried stone, forged iron and glass. They linger in a scene not of their making, awaiting further direction, their place, their home, a stage set for a story they will soon be scripted out of. They are lingering too long in the harsh light of your gaze, unwanted, perhaps, as the scene fades, the curtain drops down and invisible stagehands emerge from the wings to dismantle their surroundings. And they are left in the void, to stand in absence, of history, of memory.

I have withdrawn, and you, Eaton Manufacturing, a building, a being, are distant now, waiting beyond a cluster of other buildings, domestic hovels pressed against plank-fenced yards holding the horses that will pull the dark carts now at rest, lined up along the edge of the alley, the ground covered in softening snowpack, still rutted from yesterday's traffic. Above, the first light of dawn shines golden against your upper floors, bouncing back brilliantly off your regiment of windows, through a cool haze that will soon burn off as the day progresses. But not below, where the mist, cast in purple shadow, will linger, bodies flowing through a miasma, immersed in your breath.

I find myself north of you, past Albert Street, beyond Louisa Street, even as far as Alice Street, in a courtyard, enclosed by pale stucco structures, just southeast of the Church of the Holy Trinity, architect Henry Bowyer Lane's modest Gothic Revival structure, funded by one Mary Lambert Swale of Settle, England, who had never come to this place but wanted a holy space here, free of hierarchies, of systems of privilege, of reserved pews for the moneyed classes keeping everyone in their place. Holy

Left: Charles E. Goad, ***Atlas of the City of Toronto and Suburbs in Three Volumes: Volume Three,*** **Plate 9 (1912)**

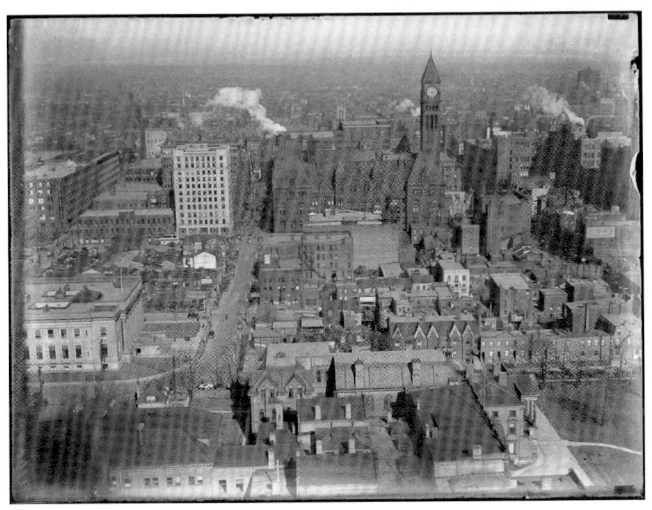

William James, View of the Ward looking east from the roof of the Canada Life Building (1910)

Trinity rose up in a city where only a decade earlier, in 1834, the Family Compact and the extensive Clergy Reserve lands had sparked a rebellion led by the firebrand and former mayor (Toronto's first) William Lyon MacKenzie, who challenged power and privilege, a protest crushed just north of here on Yonge Street, at Montgomery's Inn. John Simcoe Macaulay had given the land for this church in 1845; he gave up a cottage he had named Teraulay that sat in Macaulay's Field, on property defined by Yonge and Bay (then known as Teraulay Street), between Albert (then Jeremy) and Dundas (then Agnes). Around the church, houses rose in a little suburb called Macaulay Town that would become known as St. John's Ward, and eventually just "the Ward." All of the above happened on land purchased from the Mississauga in 1787, in a land deal that was highly disputed and revisited in 1805, and not resolved until 2010. There remains little trace of any of this, save the church where a poster within speaks of deeper memories, two long-buried creeks that once met here and were "sacred to the Mississauga."

Just to the west of Holy Trinity was another church, built two years earlier by African Methodists, Freemen and fugitive slaves who fled north out of slavery to a city home to a growing abolitionist movement. The British Methodist Episcopal Church, once an anchor for a substantial and growing Black community, no longer stands at 94 Chestnut; it is now a parking lot, soon to be a provincial courthouse, while a much diminished congregation still remains in the city.[iv] By the turn of the century there were numerous Black churches in the area, on Adelaide where the Sheraton Hotel now stands, on the site of St. Michael's Hospital at Queen and Victoria, and on the northeast corner of Agnes and Teraulay (now Dundas and Bay). The Agnes Street Methodist Church would hold its ground

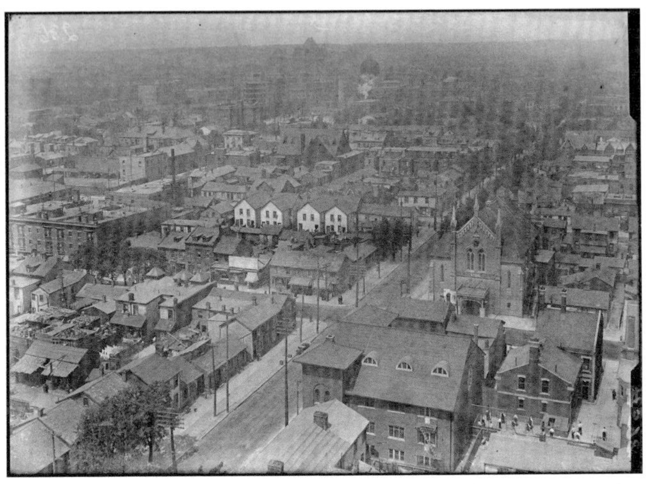

William James, View of the Ward from the roof of the Eaton Manufacturing Building looking north west; the Lyric Yiddish Theatre (former Agnes Street Methodist Church) is prominent centre right on corner of Terauley and Agnes Streets (1910)

until 1909, when the congregation sold the building to the Lyric Yiddish Theatre, a clear sign of transition in the Ward, marking the great influx of European and Jewish migrants who transformed the neighbourhood at a time when a distinct Chinese community was also just becoming established. But their collective presence on this ground would be fleeting, their bodies absented, pushed out by the forces of "progress and renewal" beginning to percolate where I now stand, in this cool, early-morning mist, gazing up at Eaton's red brick monolith now stirring to life, its inner workings powering up inside a space of both warehousing and manufacture. I can hear the Model A trucks idling on the adjacent block, machines that are steadily replacing the thousands of horses drawing carts across the city. And there, in the shadows, to the left, stands a lone figure facing away, a burlap sack slung over their shoulder as they contemplate a gap between homes, opening on to an alley that will take us out of the courtyard to Louisa Street. What's the baggage they are saddled with, their burden, their cargo? *All these absent bodies still haunt this place.*

I follow the figure with the sack down the alley and out onto Louisa Street. They turn right, heading west in the direction of Osgoode Hall now peaking above the low roofline of cottages and decaying stucco housefronts sprawling around me, expensive rented hovels owned by absentee landlords. This is not a cheap place to be. My companion is now conscious of my presence; I'm being led, and I follow. They move slowly, labouring under the weight of the sack's contents, as the massive Armoury, fronting onto University Avenue and backing onto Chestnut, looms in the distance. But I don't venture that far, as they now turn south onto Elizabeth, heading to Queen. I pass the crossroads of Elizabeth and Albert, edge by a warehouse with tall wooden hoarding around the yard. Then

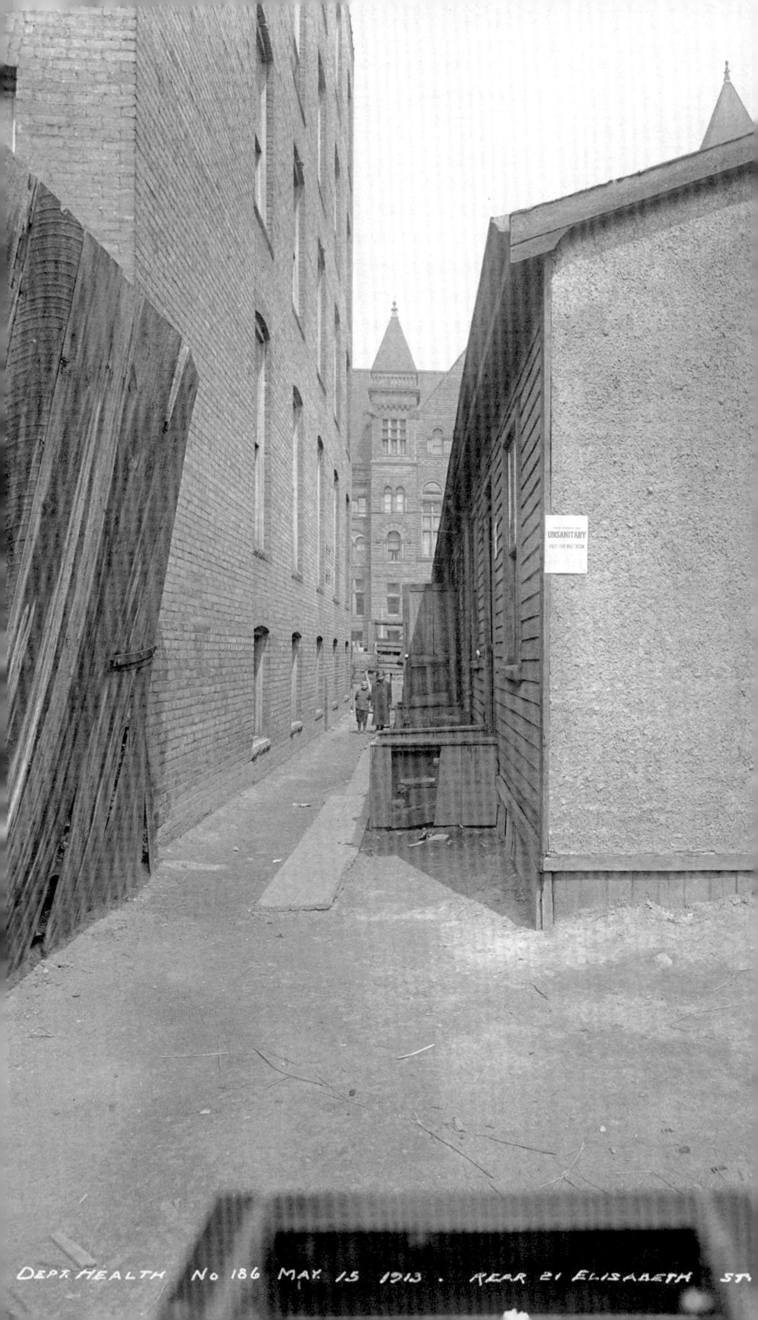
UNSANITARY
DEPT. HEALTH No 186 MAY 15 1913 . REAR 21 ELISABETH ST.

they quickly turn left, and as I come round the corner, they are gone. I now face back towards Old City Hall, its clock tower obscured by a row of houses, two children stand in the narrow alley atop wide planks laid down over dirt ground that turned to muck in the rain following the brutal, snowy winter of 1912. The children stand still, as if I am blocking their progress, afraid to come forward, and so I move away, out into a cleared patch of hard ground edged by woodsheds and a jumble of boards and broken furniture, and when I turn back towards City Hall, she is standing before me, in a long woolen coat, secured tight against the chill by two large buttons, sewn just a little off centre. She holds a package, perhaps a book, a lost history, a diary of the Ward? May 15, 1913, I am in back of Elizabeth Street, looking through Arthur Goss's lens (*see pages 22–23*).

By 1913, the Ward had come to refer to a condition as much as a place, calling up visions of "slums," sickness and "foreign" elements perceived by the WASP establishment as a threat to *Toronto the Good*. During the 1910s, the Ward was a focus of much concern due to poor housing and terrible sanitary conditions in some parts of the neighbourhood. Much of the housing was old stock, poorly built and run down, entailing serious health risks, including tuberculosis that spread easily in overcrowded homes. Arthur Goss (1881–1940) and William James (1866–1948) photographed extensively in the Ward during these years, Goss working for the City of Toronto's Department of Health, and James independently for the press. Goss in particular produced powerfully haunting images, often of lonely figures standing outside homes tagged with white paper notices declaring them condemned; forlorn and homeless bodies who would soon relocate to other parts of the growing city, to Kensington Market, to Spadina, to College and Bathurst,

Left: **Arthur Goss, Rear 21 Elizabeth Street (May 13, 1913)**

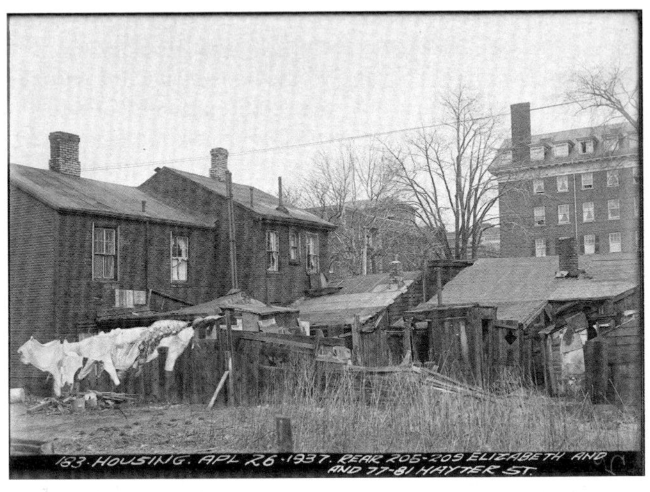

Arthur Goss, Rear 205–209 Elizabeth and 77–81 Hayter Streets (April 26, 1937)

forming the nucleuses of neighbourhood "villages" that have come to define Toronto. Yet other communities would be fragmented, their histories erased: Indigenous roots (and their continued existence) forgotten and obscured, the early Black presence disregarded as the churches vanished and the community dispersed, across Toronto and even back to the United States. (After the Civil War, there was an exodus of early Black Canadian residents south, to states like Ohio, away from the racism of Upper Canada, settlements in Canada West (Southern Ontario) emptied out. And ironically, while home to the first Abolitionist Society in Canada, Toronto was also a chosen refuge for many Confederate leaders and sympathizers.) And as Goss and James roam the neighbourhood, Lawren Harris emerges in the northeast corner of the Ward, from the Arts & Letters Club, St. George's Hall at 14 Elm Street (where it still stands), then a gentlemen's club for those who work in and "love" the arts, writers, painters, sculptors, architects, designers and actors. It was here that he would gather with his allies, the artists who would form the Group of Seven in 1920, and the writers and thinkers who would support and inform their vision of a distinct national culture and identity, grounded in a reimagining of landscape and place, an aggressively confident and prescriptive claim on the country as pure wilderness, unpeopled, untouched and without history, a space of renewal and regeneration, of whiteness, of whiteness, of whiteness...

But Harris is not moving into *that* landscape yet, that is still a few years off. He wanders the same streets as Goss, as me, as the figure with the weighted sack, as the two still children in the alley, as the lonely child with the mysterious book behind Elizabeth Street. He begins to draw and paint, searching for his subject matter, searching to find *his* voice. Like Goss he

Next: Arthur Goss, Rear of 142 Agnes Street (November 26, 1913)

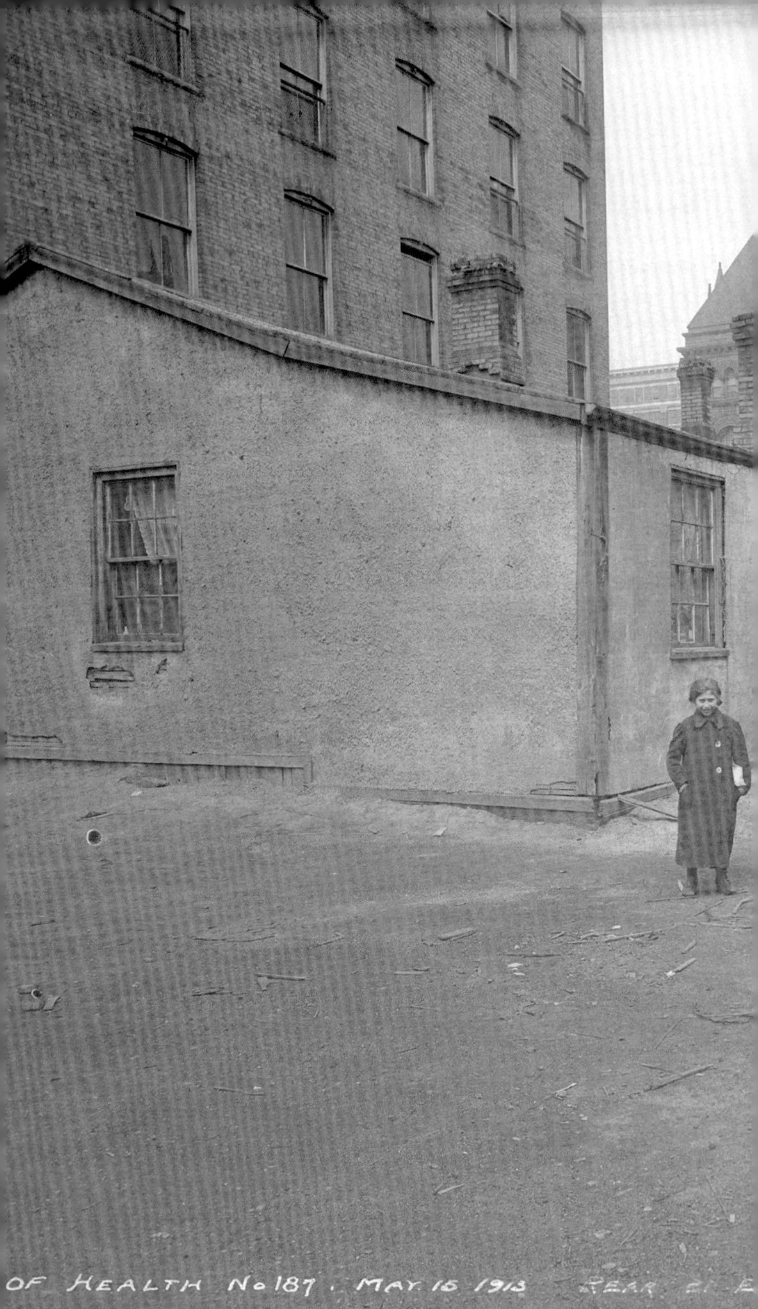
OF HEALTH No 187 . MAY 16 1913 REAR 21 E

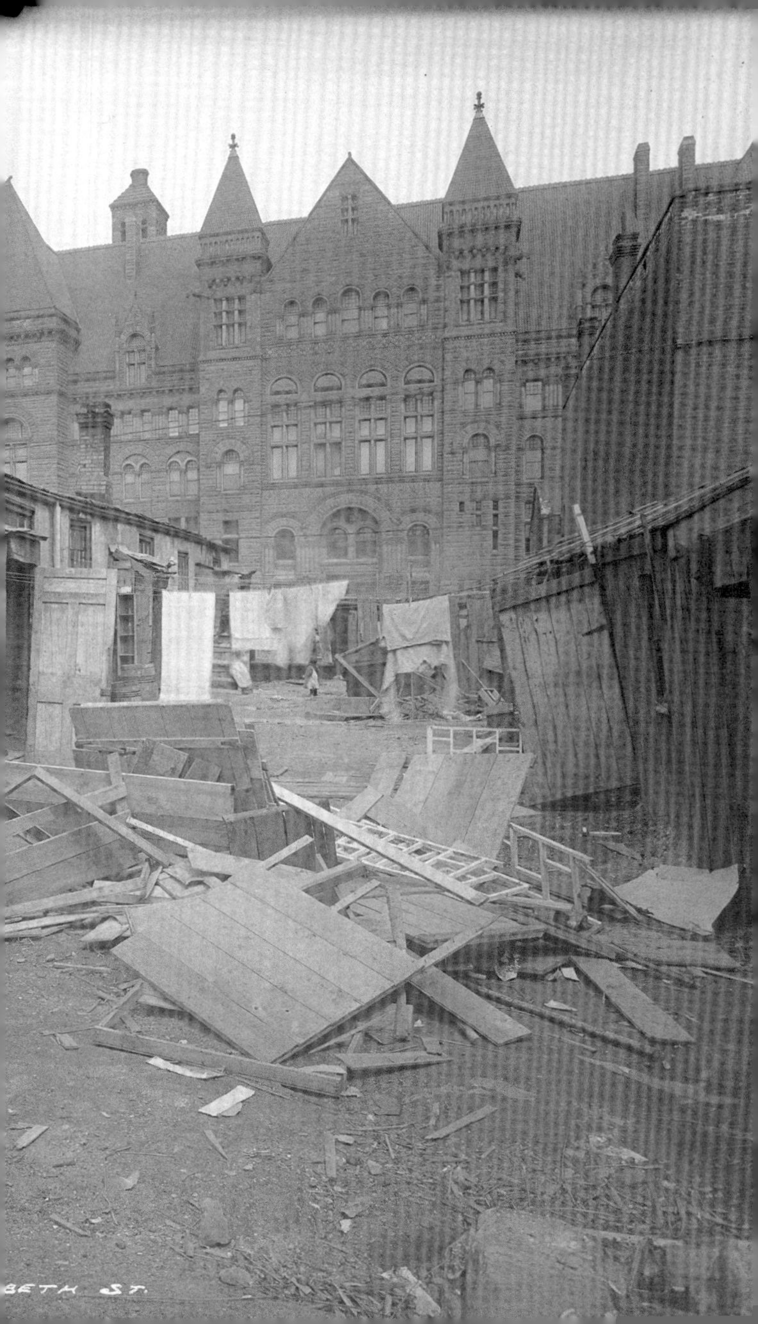
BETH ST.

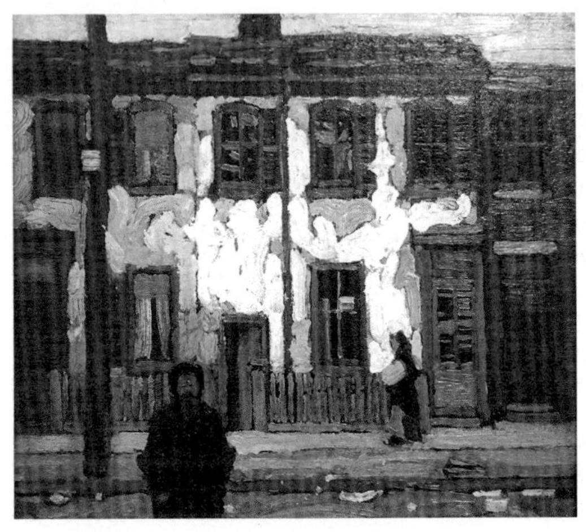

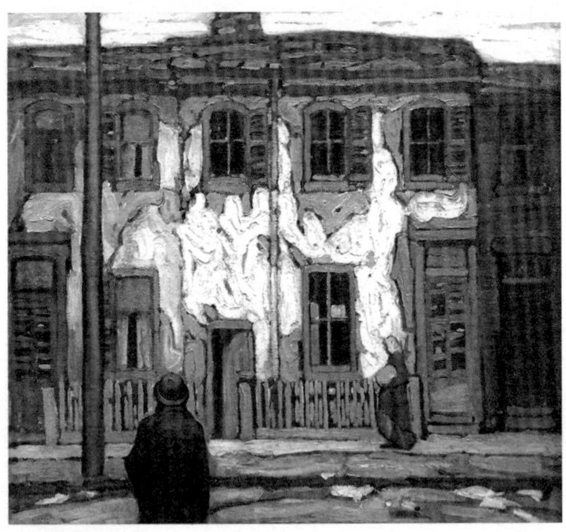

Lawren S. Harris
Upper: Sketch for *In the Ward* (1920), oil on board
Lower: *In the Ward* (1920), oil on canvas

focuses on the houses in the Ward, punctuating each scene with a limited number of obscured figures, mere placeholders, seeming less than human, not of flesh and blood, standing as design forms or pictorial elements—one can imagine them as hedges or statues, static and lacking identity, presence, and life. In the sketch for *In the Ward*, there is a lone figure in the foreground, on the left, cut off by the bottom edge of the panel. This bearded man, hands in pockets, confronts me as a being, clear vestiges of a personality, of age. Yet in the final canvas for *In the Ward*, he has been turned away, his distinct features obscured, donning a bowler hat and long coat, faceless, he has become everyman.

Harris saw the modern city as dehumanizing and lonely, an isolated crowded place, and he seems to have embodied this here, and in most of his urban paintings set in the Ward and the surrounding city, until the figures eventually disappear altogether, leaving only landscape surrounding crumbling architecture—a post-apocalyptic vision grounded in gaily coloured structures rendered in fluid impasto, the ground blanketed in the weight of winter. And he would come to question this state, even as he progressed out into nature. As his colleagues fully embraced a vision of Canada as nature, a nationalist narrative that still persists, Harris was moving beyond this. A mere physical relocation, into the wilderness was not enough; he was looking for something higher, loftier, transcendent and transformative. And how could that *not* have emerged in such a space as the Ward, a place of deep spiritual resonance for so many of its inhabitants, whether Indigenous, African Methodist, Baptist, Chinese, Jewish, Mystical, or Visionary. A space of magic, of mysteries, of wonders, and also of misery—but where to go, *where to go*, to find a path forward out of the bleak, vibrant urban sadness?

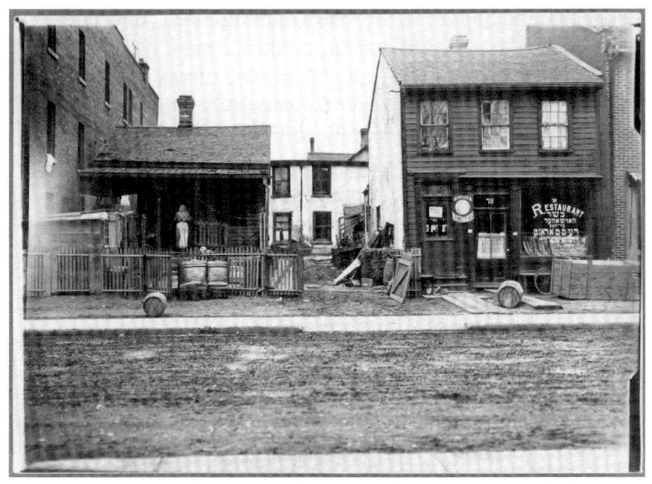

William James, Chicken Warehouse, Agnes Street (1910)

A Question

Are you like that?
Are you sad walking down streets,
Streets hard as steel; cold repellent cruel?
Are you sad seeing people there,
Outcast from beauty,
Even afraid of beauty,
Not knowing?

Are you sad when you look down city lanes,
Lanes littered with ashes, boxes, canes, old rags;
Dirty, musty, garbage-reeking lanes
Behind the soot-dripped backs of blunt houses,
Sour yards and slack sagging fences?

When you see great cities,
Jagged squares of baked clay, and steel and stone,
Canals of filth under every street,
Smoke-breathed, din-shrouded,
Seething with blind, driven people—
Seeing pilgrims settling down in the earth's scum,
In mud,
Feeling sin,
Are you sad?
Are you like that?

— LAWREN HARRIS, *A QUESTION* (1922)[v]

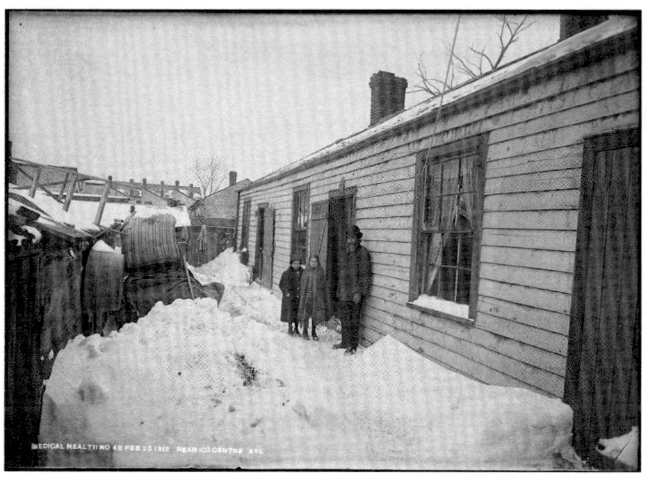

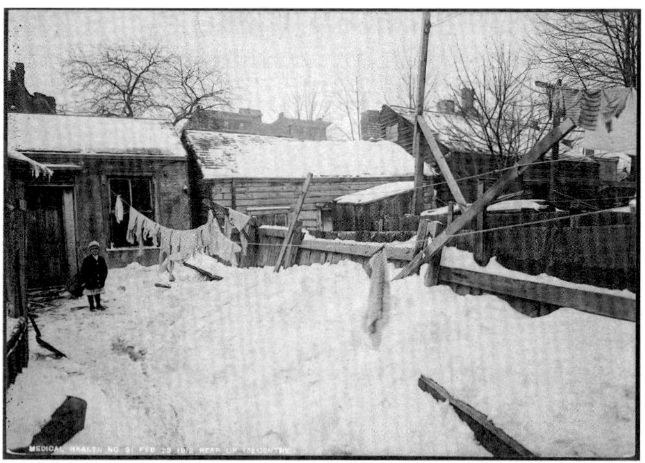

Arthur Goss
Upper: Rear of 102 Centre Street (February 23, 1912)
Lower: Rear of 152 Centre Street (February 23, 1912)

Such a *Grey Day in Town*, the weather has turned cold again, the snow falls, not picturesquely blanketing the ground, but falling heavy, in wet lumps and clusters, to burden the earth, cold and damp. We've moved back in time to February 1912, to travel once again with Goss, along Chestnut Street and Centre Avenue, Christopher, Alice, Louisa and Albert, then on to Elizabeth. A frigid wind blows in off the lake, penetrating every layer of garment, some shrouding themselves in blankets atop overcoats as they once again stand outside of homes condemned, forced to move on, but where? An aged, bearded man stands leaning against pale clapboard, facing us, sporting a bowler hat (is this Harris's man from *In the Ward?*) and accompanied by two young girls, one shrouded in a woolen blanket. Nearby, a pile of detritus topped by a folded mattress, at rest, piled high against a long arch of woodsheds and railings, speaks of eviction.

Centre Avenue, one block east of University, near Dundas. The snow is deep and thick, feeding on the footings of a house row. Further up this street, a backyard of deep, hardened drifts, caressed by thinning laundry hung to dry (more likely to freeze), jury-rigged timbers prop up other wires and line the ground, perhaps the edge of a summer garden, bare trees and the top floor of more comfortable lodgings protruding in the distance along University. There is a young girl positioned on the path, hindering my entrance to the cottage. At another house, two small boys guard a double door (*see page 30*) and later, back on Chestnut, I peer down an alley, the snow coated with dirt and rock debris, a man in the distance rests one leg up on a step, more laundry lingers stiff in the wind, and a mound to the right appears placed, not random; there is something beneath the

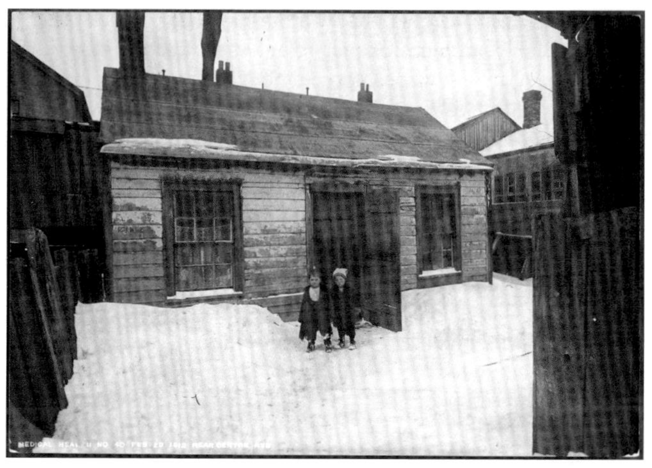

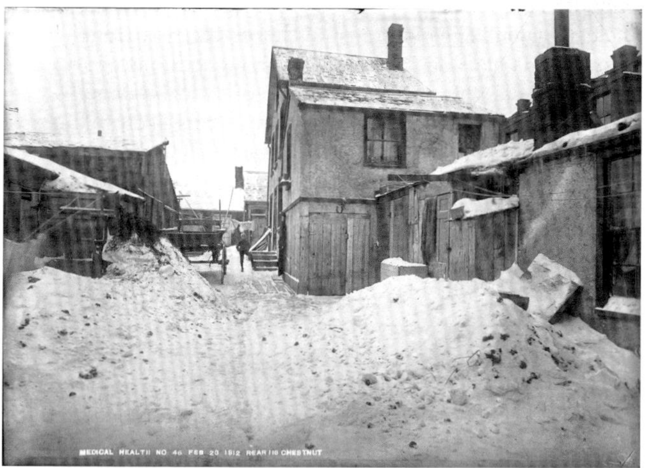

Arthur Goss
Upper: Rear of 116 Chestnut Street (February 23, 1912)
Lower: Rear of Centre Avenue (February 23, 1912)

snow cover, as if buried, a distinctly formed body of earth, the remains of a building or once excavated ground? Later, we'll return to this excavation (*see page 30 lower*).

I revisit Elizabeth Street, another one-storey shack sinking into the snow, the roof slanting, to the left a jumble of sheds cluster together as if for warmth. And there he stands, a Black gentleman framed in the doorway (*see page 32-33*). How many generations here? Did he attend the British Methodist Episcopal Church or hear the choir at the Agnes Street Methodist Church? Did he know the names of another *Group of Seven*, the group of seven Black women lost in time? (*see page 34*) Did his ancestors come north, following the North Star to freedom, like the fugitive slaves Lucie and Thornton Blackburn who started Toronto's first cab company, befriended by wealthy civic leaders like George Brown and George Gooderham (of Gooderham & Worts Distillery), owned cottages in the Ward, helped build the Little Trinity Church on King East and attended the North American Convention of Colored Freemen at St. Lawrence Hall in September 1851? This man gazes back at me, his head cocked slightly to the right. This subtle gesture, combined with the angle of view and the position of the photographer (distant, withdrawing), suggests that I am moving away from him, and yet he continues to make the effort to hold eye contact for as long as possible, until I pass out of sight, watching me escape a difficult conversation, about a past I am implicated in and that challenges comfortable narratives of being here—in this neighbourhood, in this city.

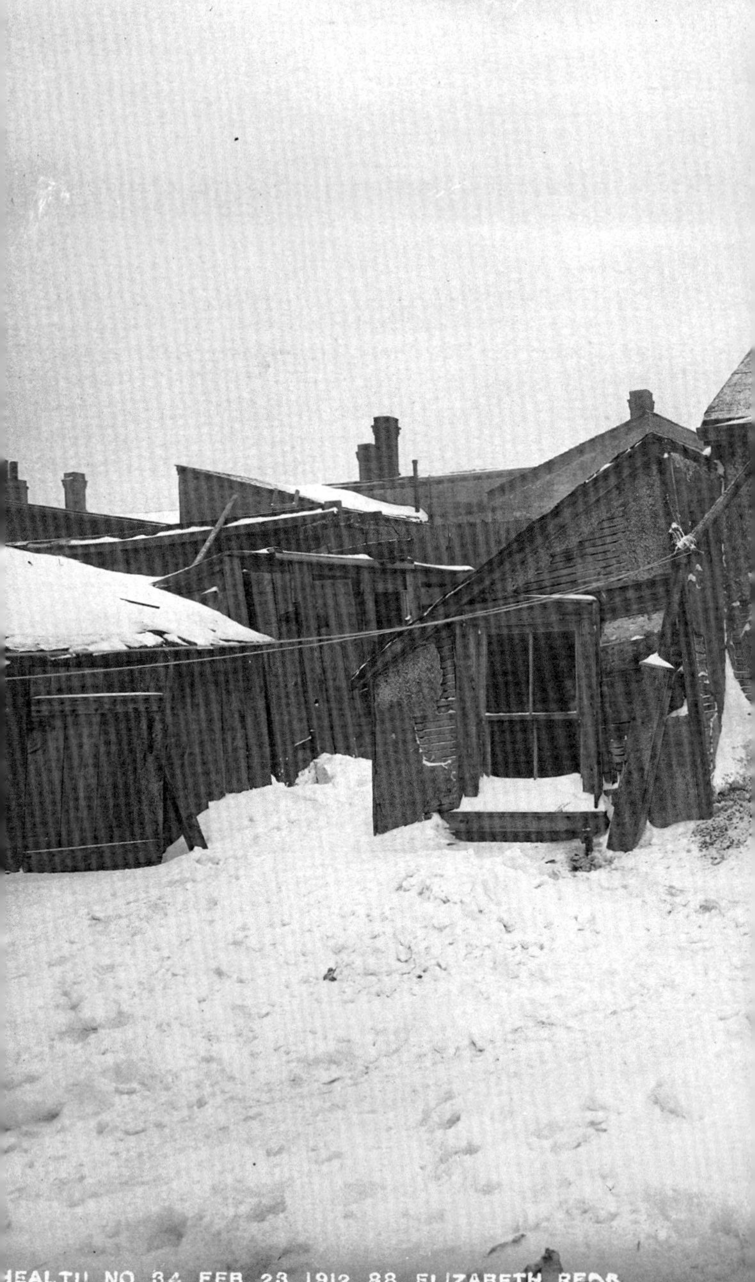
HEALTH NO 34 FEB 23 1912 88 ELIZABETH REAR

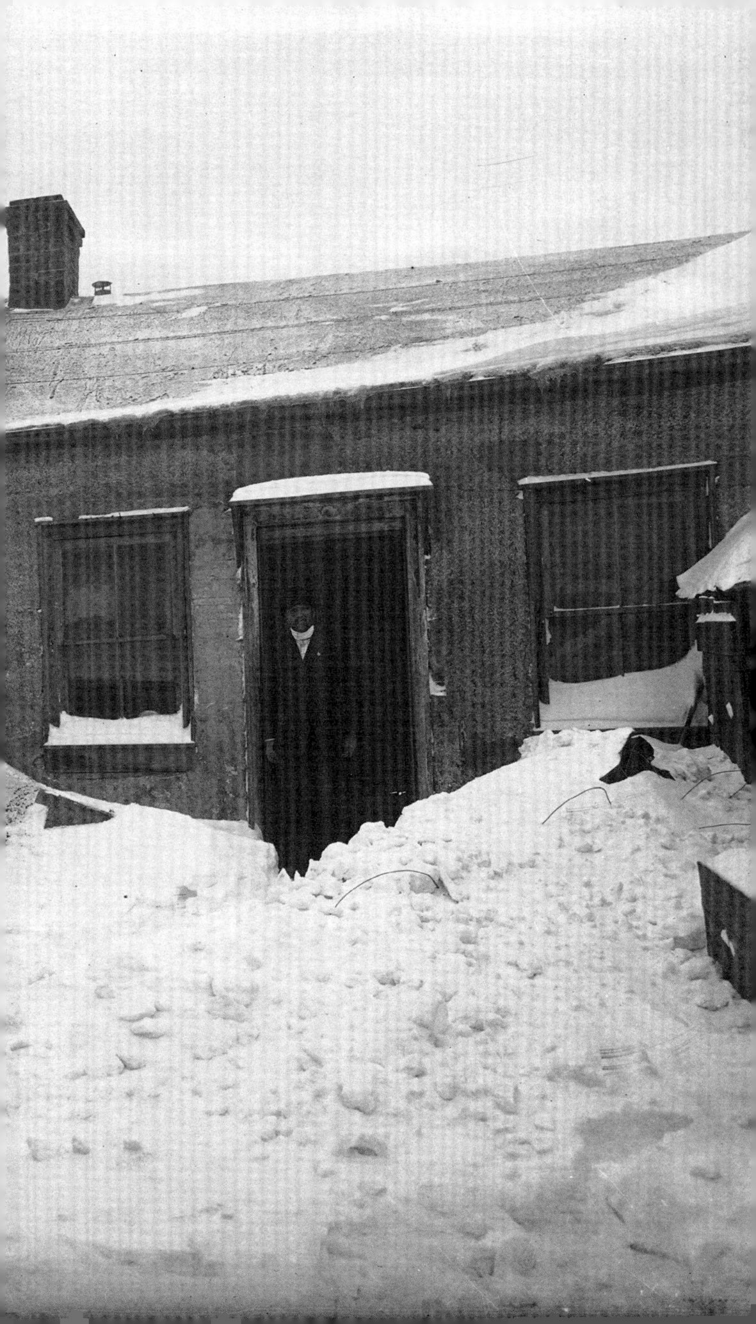

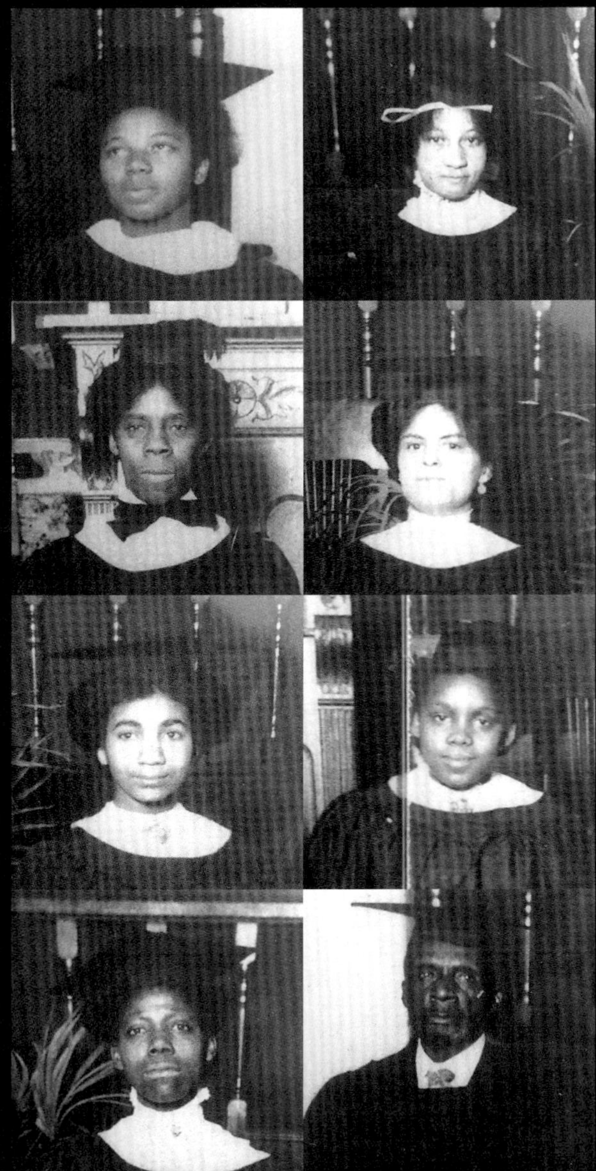

I sighed for liberty; but the bondsman's chain was round me, and could not be shaken off. I could only gaze wistfully towards the North, and think of the thousands of miles that stretched between me and the soil of freedom, over which a black freeman may not pass.

— SOLOMON NORTHUP, *TWELVE YEARS A SLAVE* (1853)[vi]

I just taught a course on Canadian Slavery. All of my students started the course with something in common—zero knowledge that slavery had occurred in Canada... Although ignorant about Canadian Slavery, my students had been schooled from a young age in the Underground Railroad which positioned Canadians as liberators of African-American Slaves. By the way, the Underground Railroad lasted from 1834 until 1865. Is something off here? How is it that we Canadians all seem to know about a three-decade window when enslaved Africans fled from the U.S.A., but we know nothing about a two hundred plus year expanse of time when we too were slaving?

— CHARMAINE NELSON, *HUFFINGTON POST* (2013)[vii]

Left: Unknown photographer, Members of the Agnes Street Methodist Church Choir, c. 1900
Previous: Arthur Goss, 88 Elizabeth Rear (February 23, 1912)

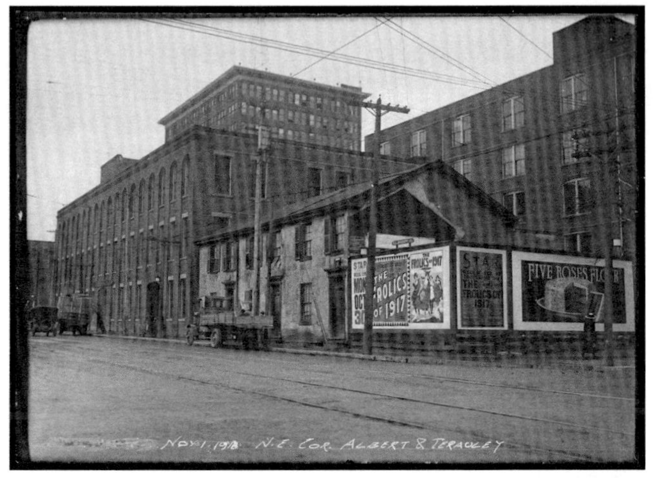

Arthur Goss, N.E. Corner of Albert and Terauley [Bay] (November, 1913)

I travel past more vacant row houses, a bleak journey through desperation. But then again, Harris, the outsider, found that there might be joy here, in a bright red door on "a gloomy house of broken grey rough-cast." "But the street door smiles," he said, "even laughs, when the hazy sunlight falls on it—Someone had painted it a bright gay red."[viii] In his expressive paintings, his first truly confident art works, Harris reminds us of a vivacity in the Ward, and in his sole attempt at published poetry in 1922, he evokes the sounds and smells of the neighbourhood, revealing that he is striving to capture more than just an image, offering up a poetic contrast to Goss's stark, black-and-white, analytical imagery.

Yet Goss the documentarian made a distinct effort to include the people, to capture them as real, as living and breathing sentient beings that belong. His characters appear as a defiant presence in so many of his images, not mere props or pictorial elements, giving us potent details that reveal the complexities of life in the neighbourhood; they are strong acknowledgments of the lives unseen by the powers that be, the stern architects of corrective measures being planned, and of those to come. Children are prominent in Goss's imagery on the streets and in the Elizabeth Street Playground located where hospitals now stand (*see page 45*). He offers details of the thriving businesses, the contrasting Chinese and Yiddish texts on the windows of adjacent businesses (*see page 38*), signage for tailors who will soon transform Spadina into the garment district, a cartoon chicken for a butcher. The Ward was alive, complex and visceral. I imagine the sound of patrons in that butcher shop, the smell of poultry being prepared, of blood running from the chopping block onto sawdust scattered over wood flooring; out front, the rattle of the streetcars and

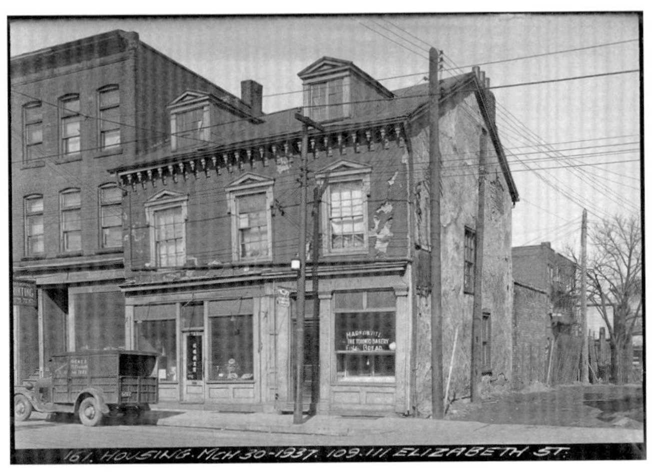

Arthur Goss, 109–111 Elizabeth Street (March 30, 1937)

peddlers, voices speaking in dozens of languages and dialects, groups of children roaming in clusters throughout the area, finding joy and adventure in any circumstance, outside of home. But the city saw the neighbourhood as a blight, a threat to civic order, a dangerous place of alien voices, strange languages and beliefs, a fertile terrain of subversion. It had to be transformed and assimilated. It had to go. This movement began in earnest during Harris's time, gaining force and momentum, and it is here that Harris's path appears to diverge.

For decades afterwards, through the Great Depression and World War Two, the Ward would be emptied out, leaving a network of haunted spaces, save for the thriving Chinatown, its main artery being Elizabeth Street running from Queen to Dundas. Harris remained a Toronto resident through 1934, but his art became all about elsewhere, his forays extending north and east, to Algonquin and Algoma, to the miners' houses at Glace Bay, and into the heart of Halifax's Africville (in his *Elevator Court* and *The Black Court* paintings). Harris mourns over the grave loss of potential, embodies the post-traumatic stress of the Great War following the loss of his brother in the trenches, and the grinding toll the city and industry have taken on the human body, mind and spirit. While Toronto chose urban renewal as the path to a bright and modern future, Harris looked away, beyond a grounded human existence, out of the dense urban space, towards nature and beyond. He did not see a future in the city, at least not a positive or progressive one, but rather aspired to transcend the here and now; like Frankenstein's monster, traumatized by the machines of the modern world, he chose a northern path, a path to some distant, imaginary truth, towards an *Idea of North*.

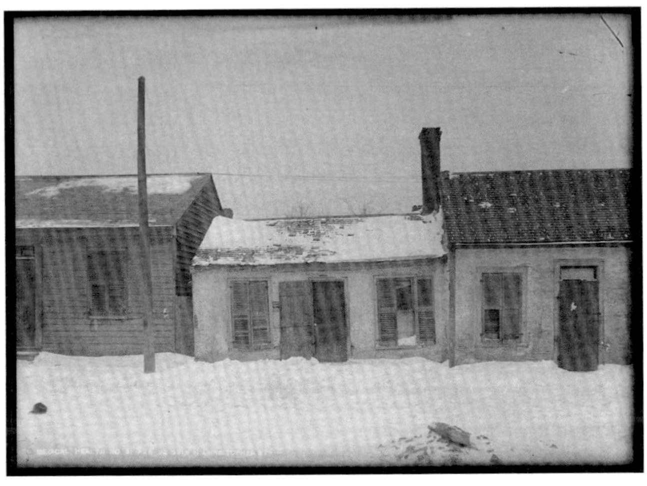

Arthur Goss, 11 Christopher Street (Febuary 23, 1912)

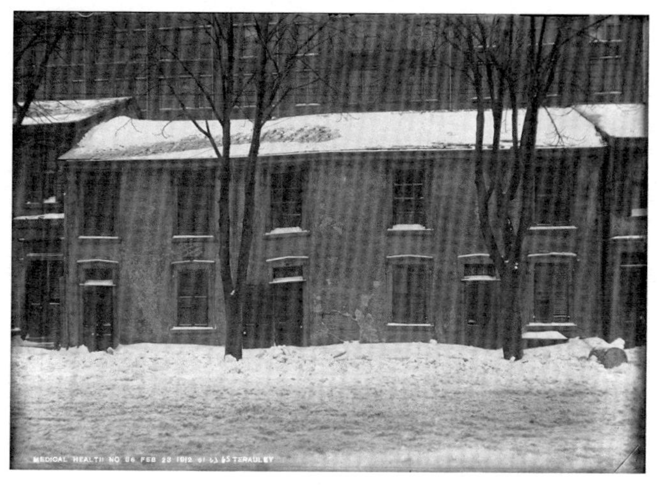

Arthur Goss, 61, 63, 65 Terauley Street (February 23, 1912)

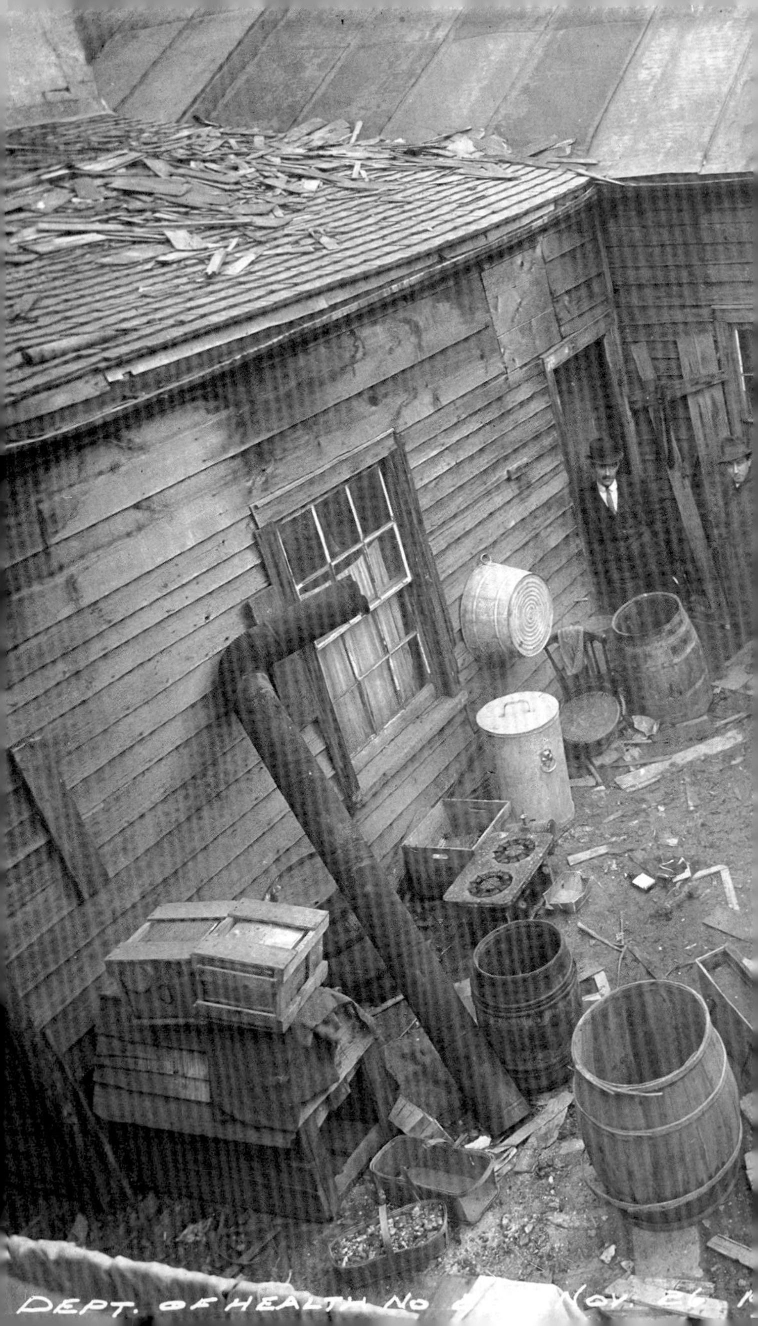
DEPT. OF HEALTH NO
NOV. 26

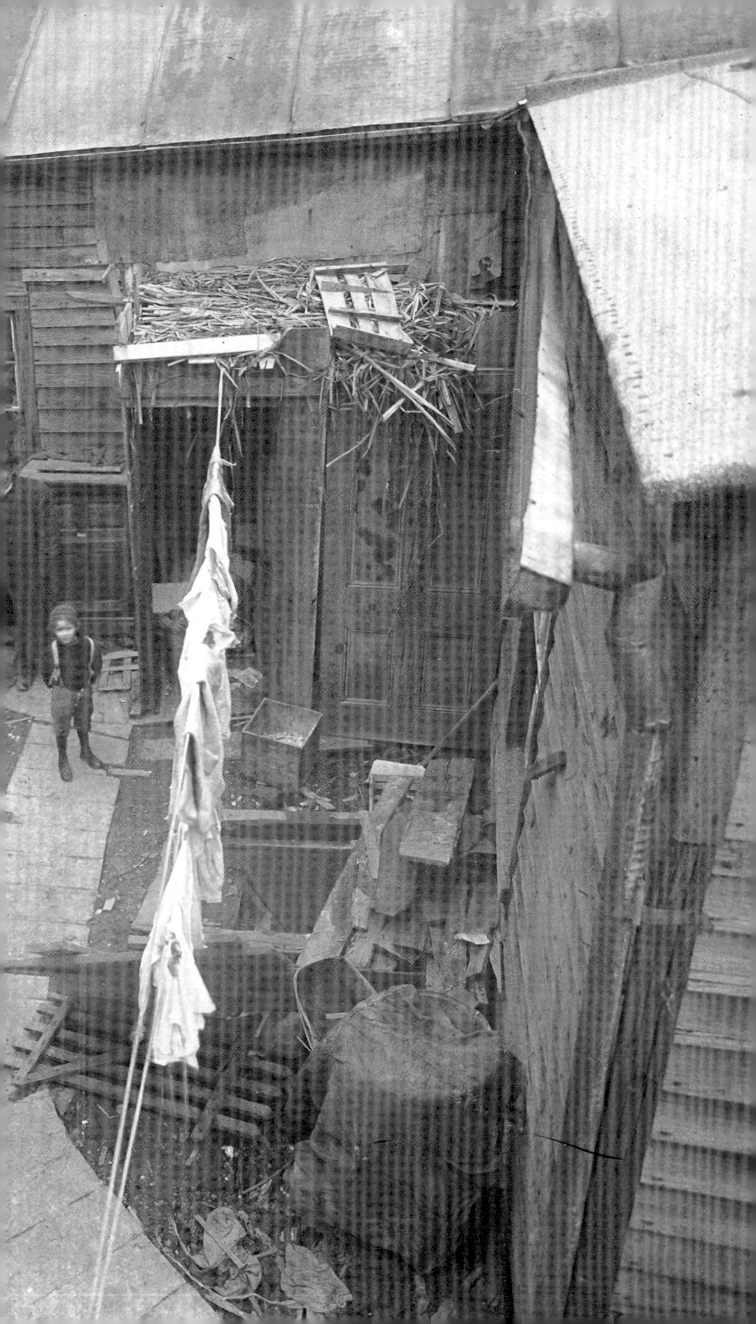

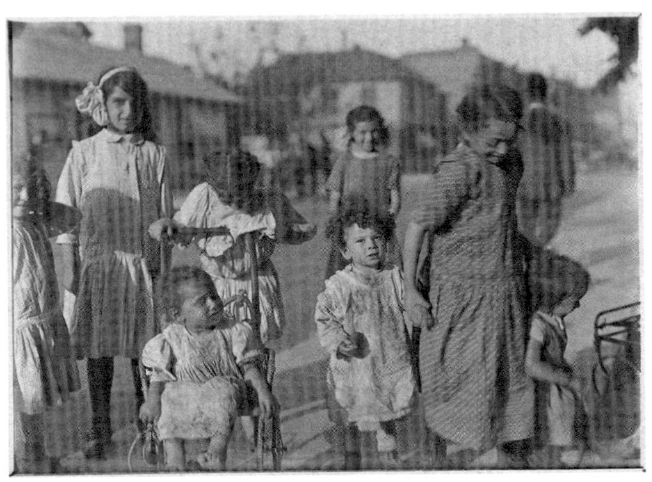

William James, Children in the Ward (1911)

Previous: Arthur Goss, Rear 21 Elizabeth Street (May 15, 1913)

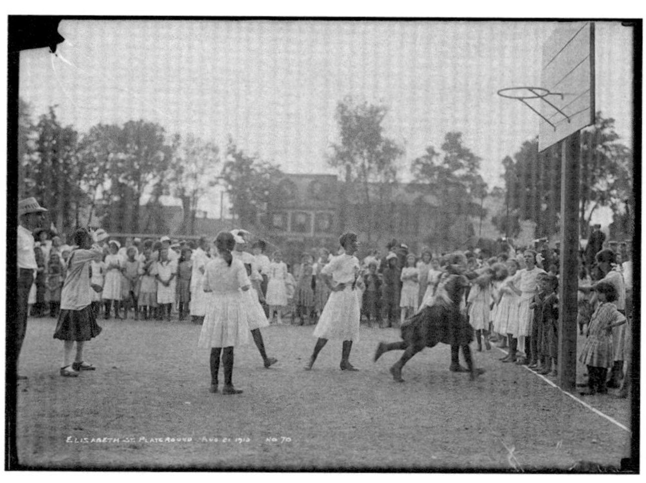

Arthur Goss, Elizabeth Street Playground (August 21, 1913)

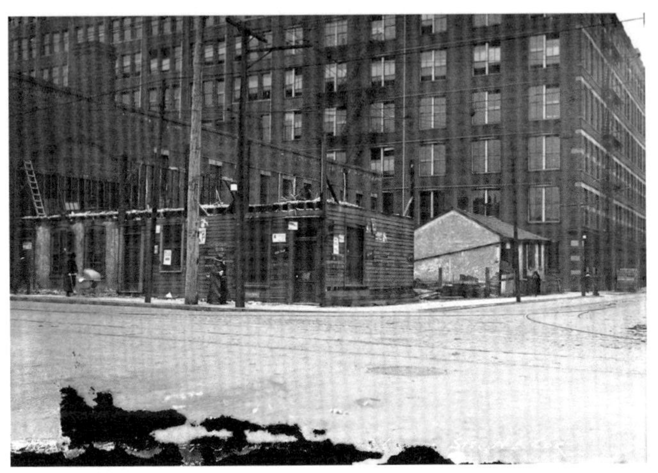

Arthur Goss, Corner of Terauley and Albert (1913)

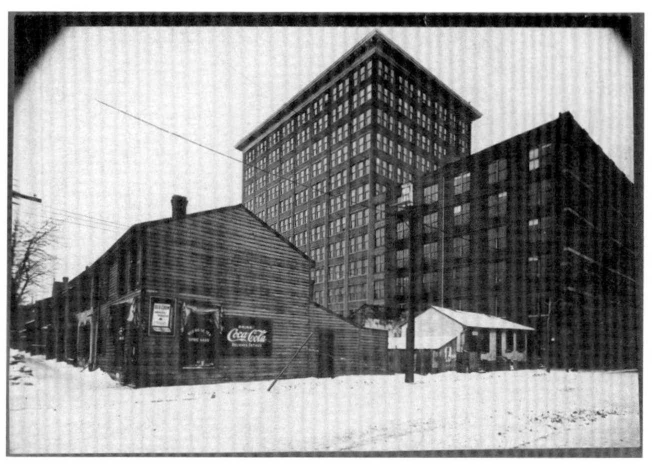

Arthur Goss, Corner of Terauley and Louisa (1913)

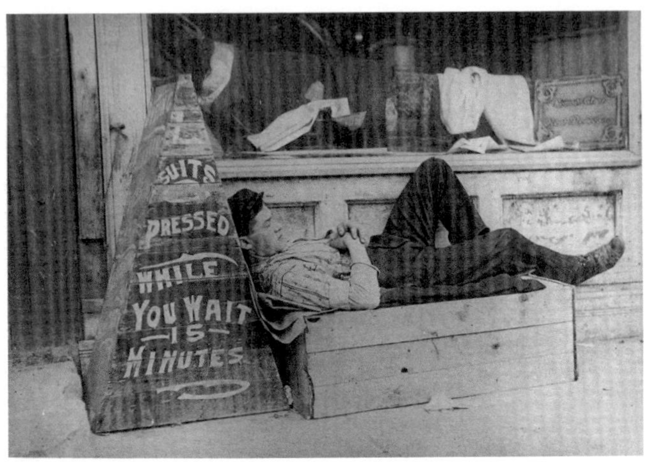

Arthur Goss, Suits Pressed While You Wait (1912)

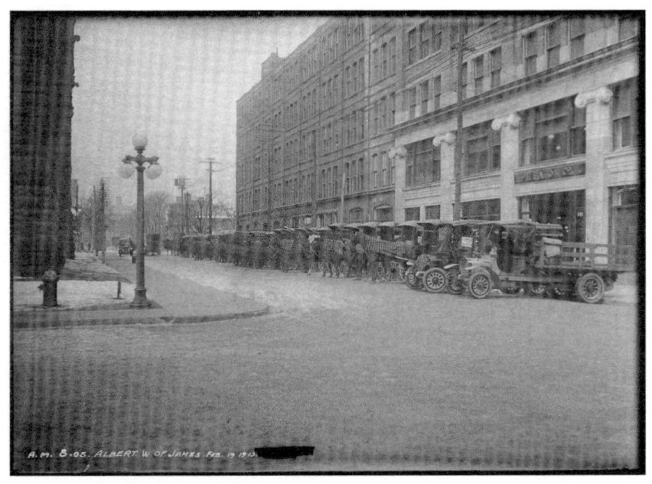

Arthur Goss, Albert Street west from James Street T.E. Eaton Company Mail Order Delivery Wagons (February 19, 1913)

Next: Arthur Goss, Santa Claus with Children (1913)

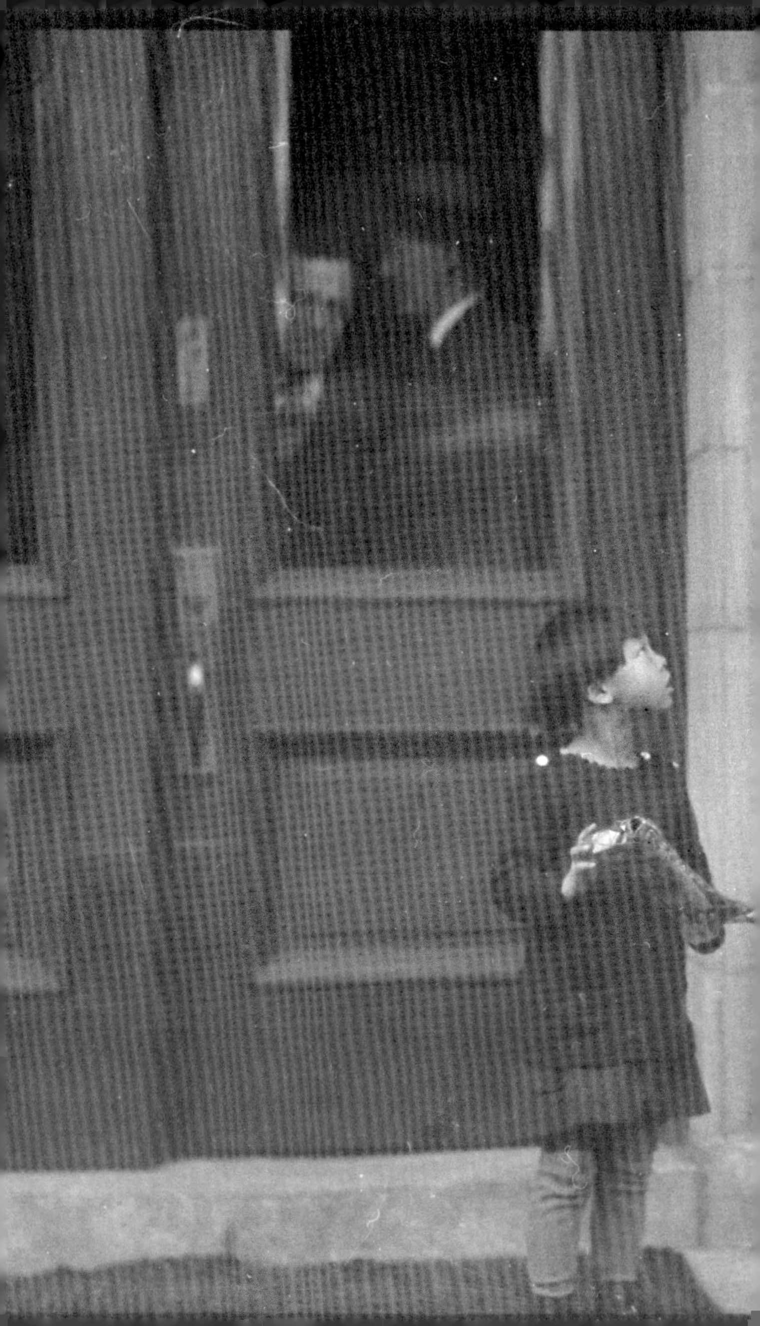

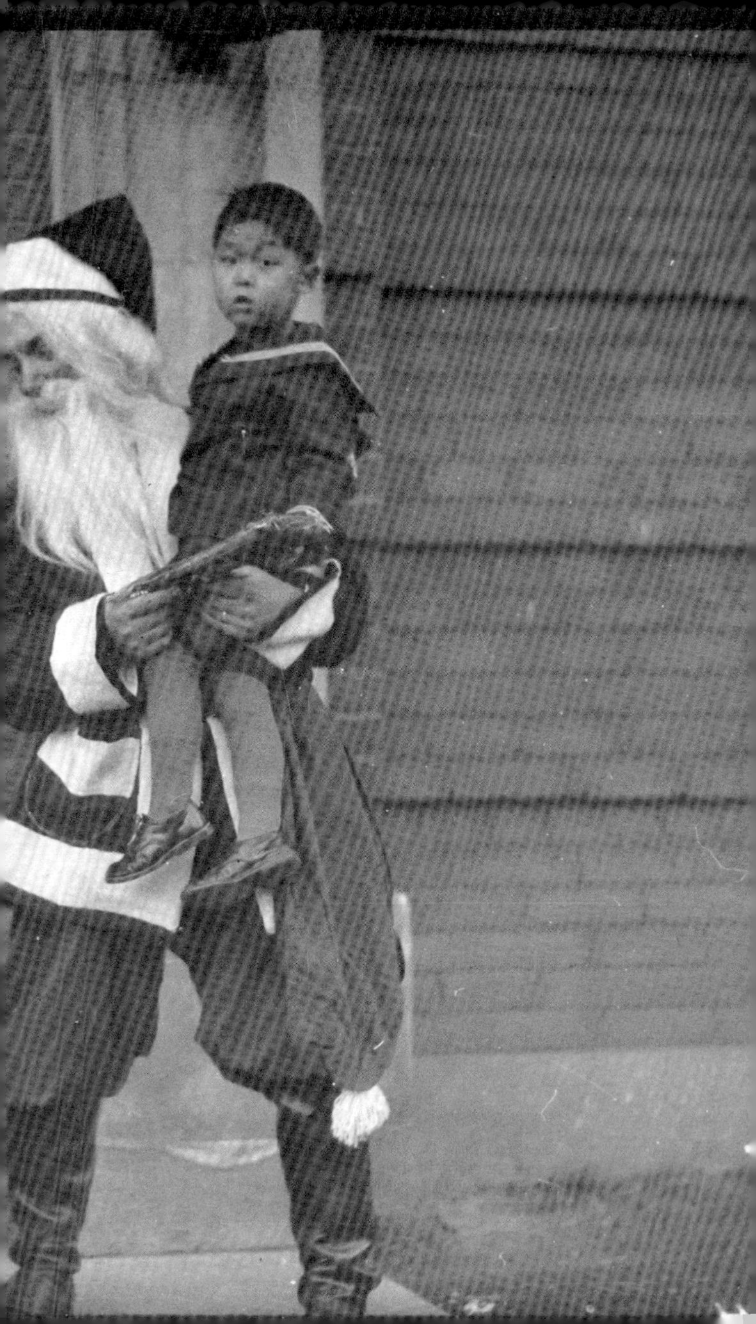

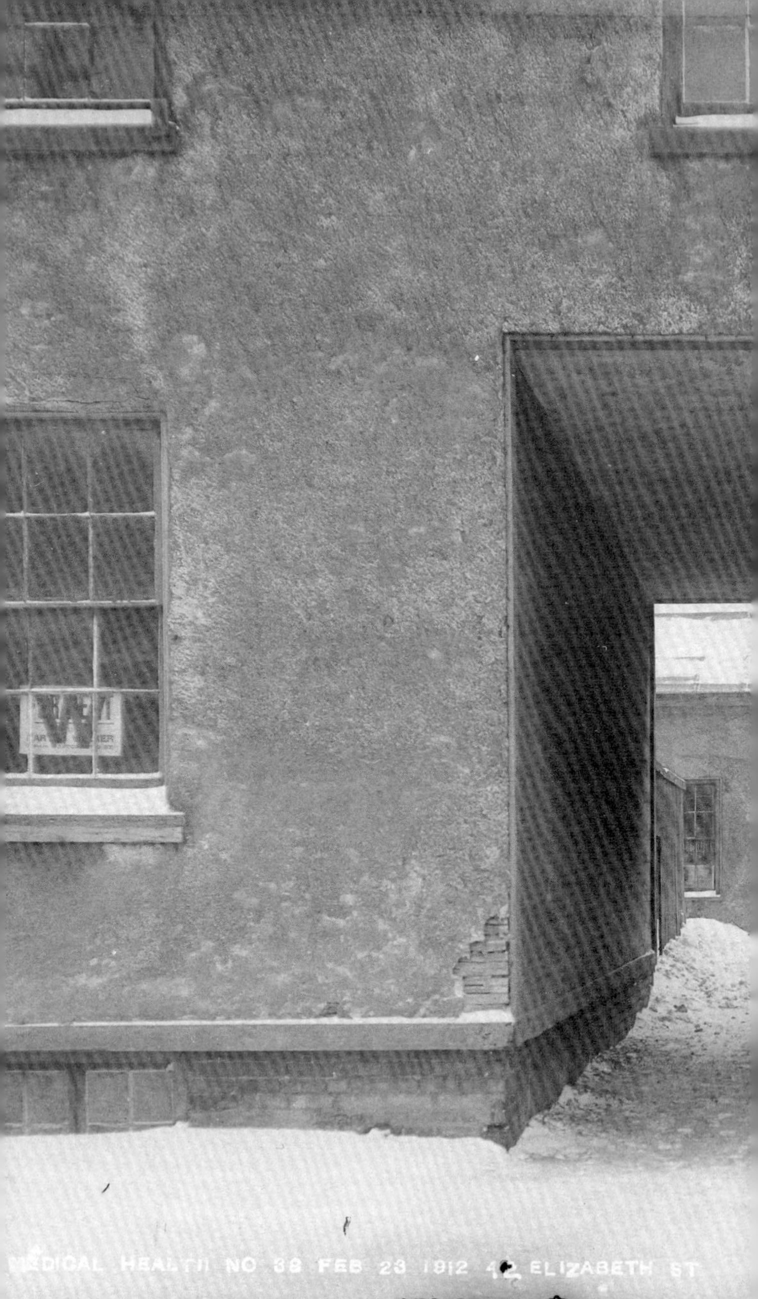
MEDICAL HEALTH NO 38 FEB 23 1912 42 ELIZABETH ST

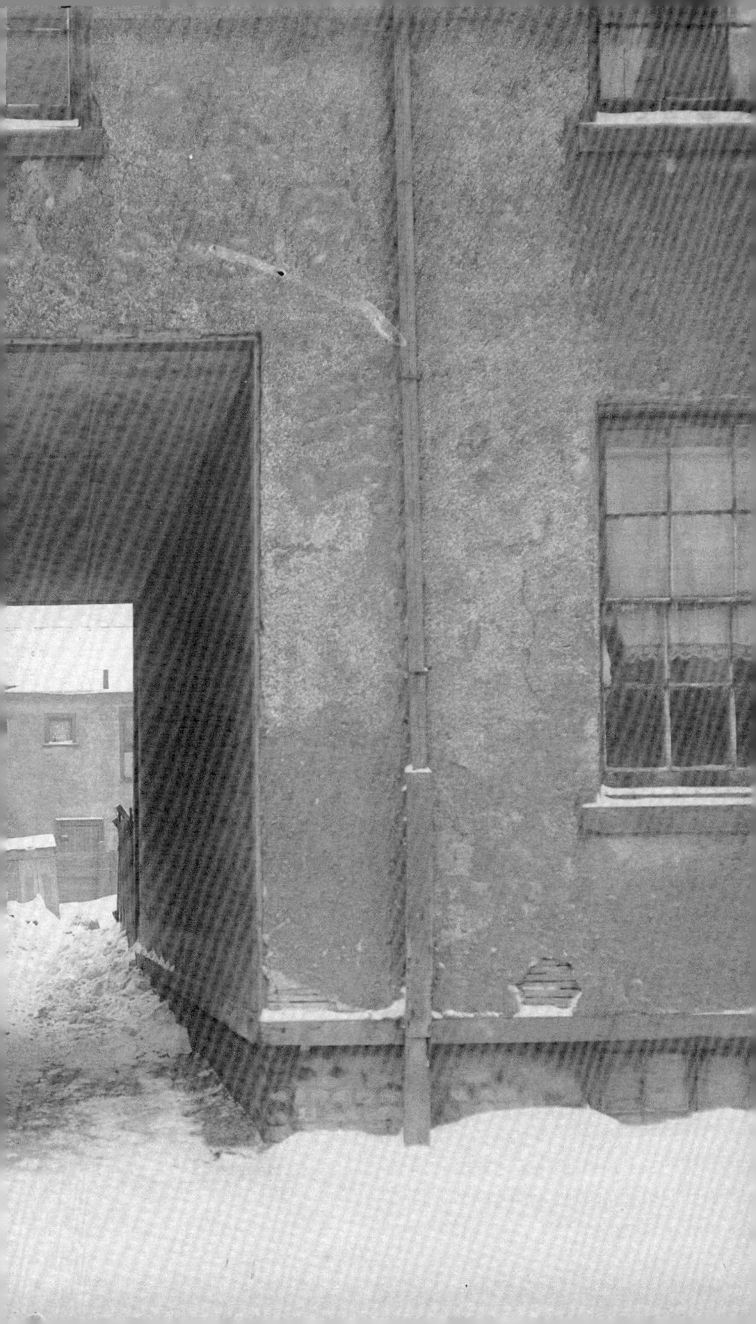

Previous: Arthur Goss, 42 Elizabeth Street (February 23, 1912)

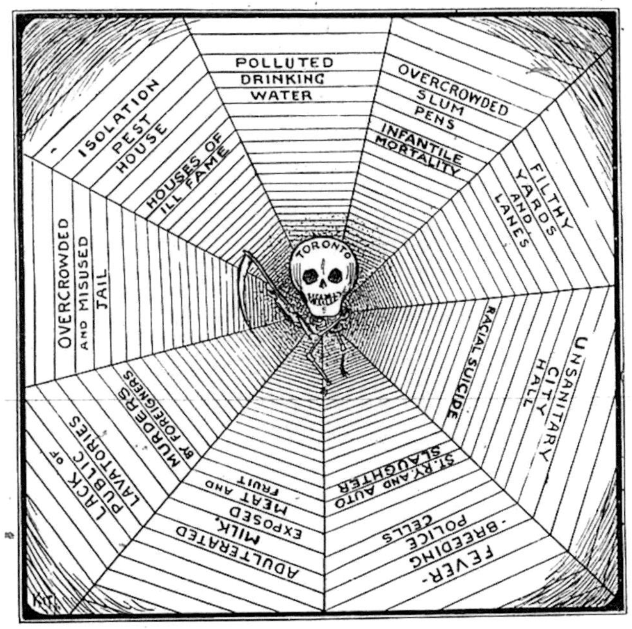

Unknown cartoonist, "Toronto?," published in *Jack Canuck* (1913)

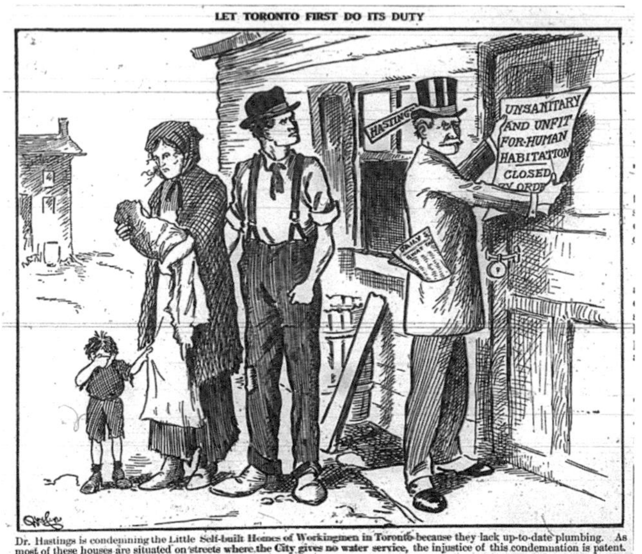

Unknown cartoonist, "Let Toronto First Do Its Duty," published in *Jack Canuck* (1913)

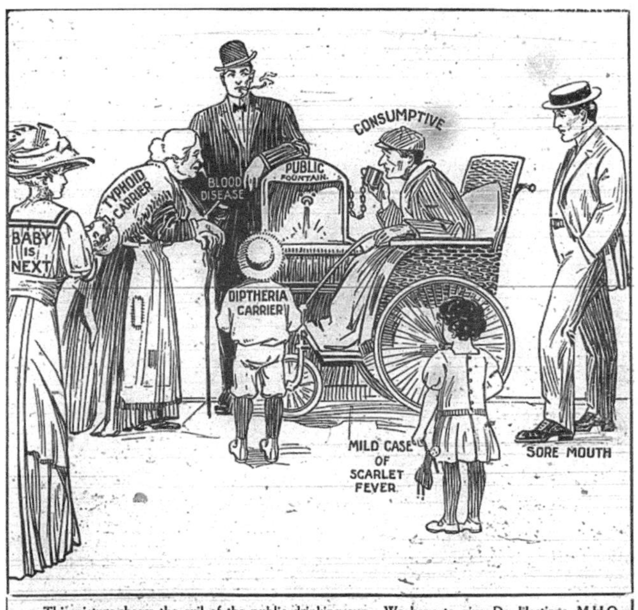

This picture shows the evil of the public drinking cup. We have to give Dr. Hastings, M.H.O., credit for the efforts he has made to abolish this filthy practice. Many cities in Canada should follow the advice of Toronto's M.H.O., and make the use of the drinking cup a criminal offence.

Unknown cartoonist, "The Evil of the Public Drinking Cup," published in *Jack Canuck* (1913)

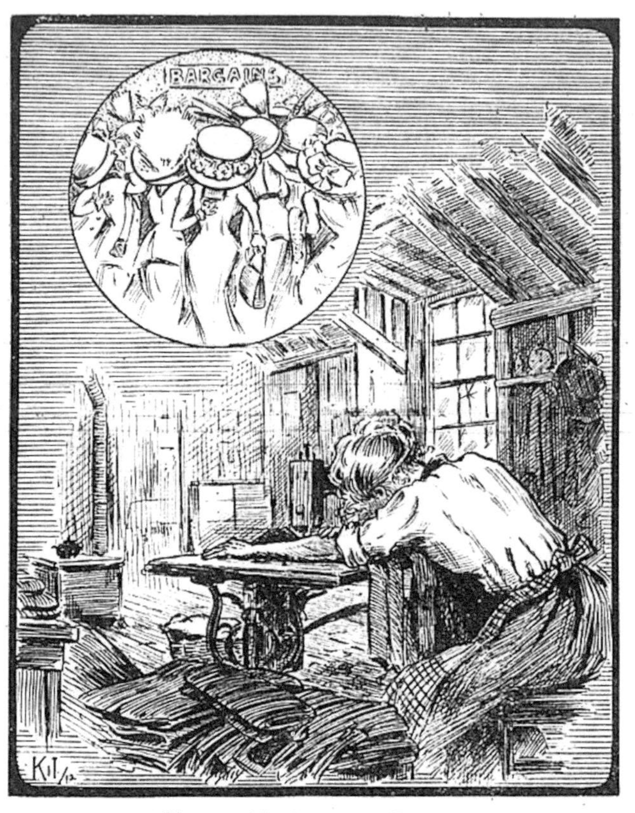

"Give us this day our daily bread."

Unknown cartoonist, "Give Us This Day Our Daily Bread," published in *Jack Canuck* (1913)

QUEEN CITY'S CONCEPTION OF BEAUTY

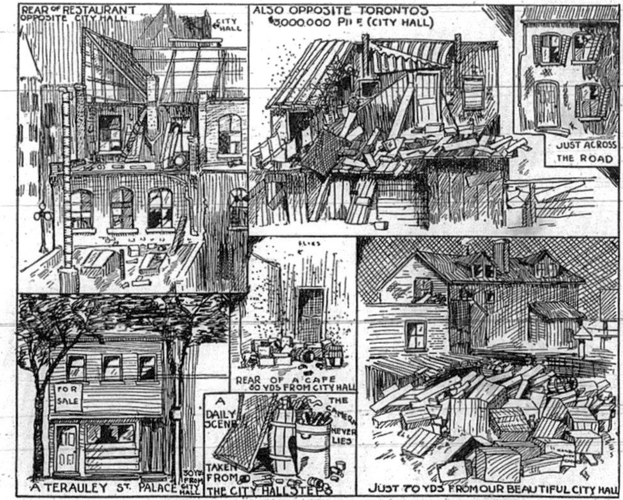

This is Scenery in the immediate vicinity of Toronto's City Hall. It is quite normal. There has been no cyclone. Dr. Hastings might have noticed the same, but he is too busy counting flies to help the T. Eaton Company, via the "Star," to sell fly traps.

Unknown cartoonist, "Queen City's Conception of Beauty," published in *Jack Canuck* (1913)

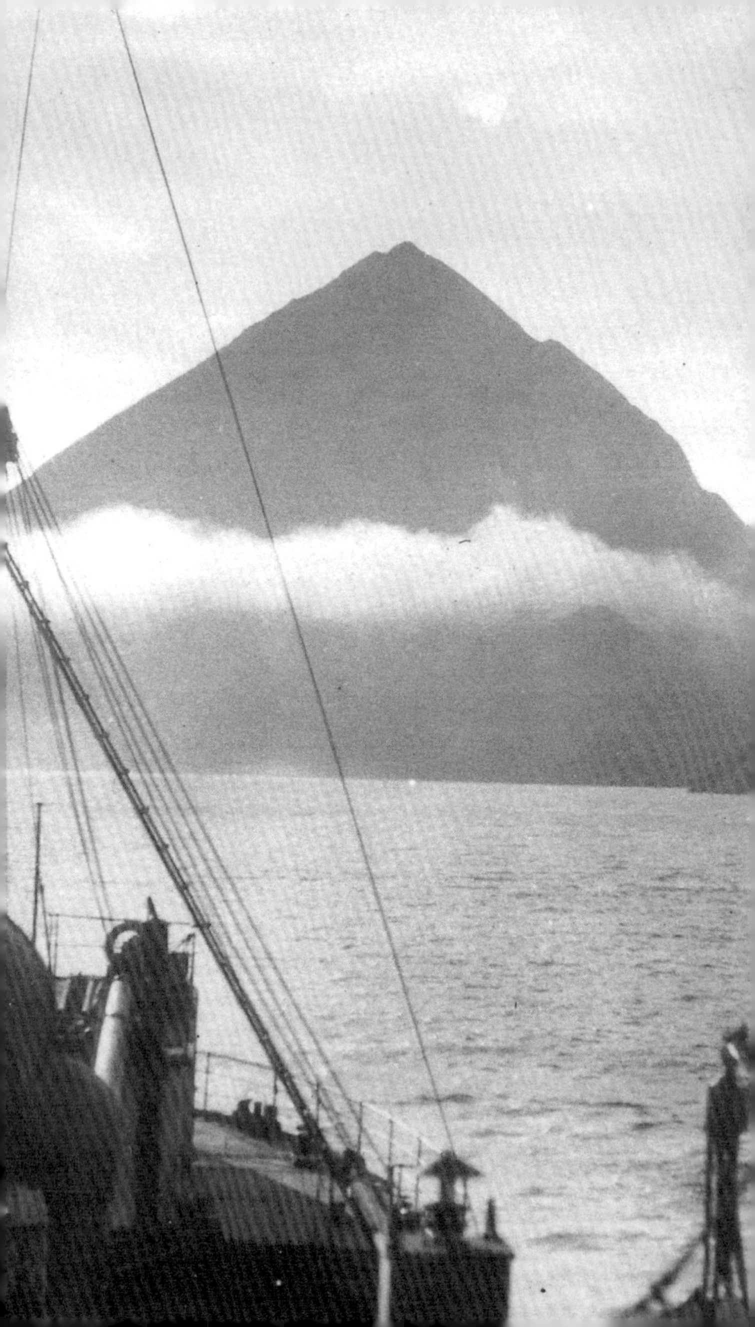

Part 2
In the North

The ship pushes on through open water, only occasionally approaching some drifting iceberg or the loose break-up of winter pack ice. Harris has ventured into the far north, with fellow Group of Seven artist A.Y. Jackson, heading out from Halifax, touching on Newfoundland, then through Arctic waters (Hudson and Davis Straits, Lancaster and Jones Sounds, and Baffin Bay), even visiting Godhaven in western Greenland. He is aboard the *S.S. Beothic*, a rugged sealing vessel leased annually by the Canadian government to take supplies north to RCMP posts and government researchers on annual field-work. Jackson had travelled north on the same vessel in 1927, accompanied by scientist and artist Dr. Frederick N. Banting (co-discoverer of Insulin, for which he received the Nobel prize in 1923). In 1930 it was Harris's turn to venture on his sole Arctic call. By then, he was well along his chosen path, progressing on a spiritual journey in search of a different temporal plane of knowledge. He had begun to map this out in his earlier paintings from Lake Superior's north shore, gazing out over the deep, dark waters raked by sheets of northern light, and in his pictorial inventions based on the snow-capped Rocky Mountains, with their ancient glaciers, dense frozen masses that flow imperceptibly, far beyond the rhythms of human movement. Those sharp cuts on the mountain forms, with their rounded foothills, speak of a deep history of glaciation to those aware of these forces. In so many of Harris's paintings,

Left: Lawren S. Harris, View from the Deck of the S.S. Beothic, Eastern Arctic (1930)

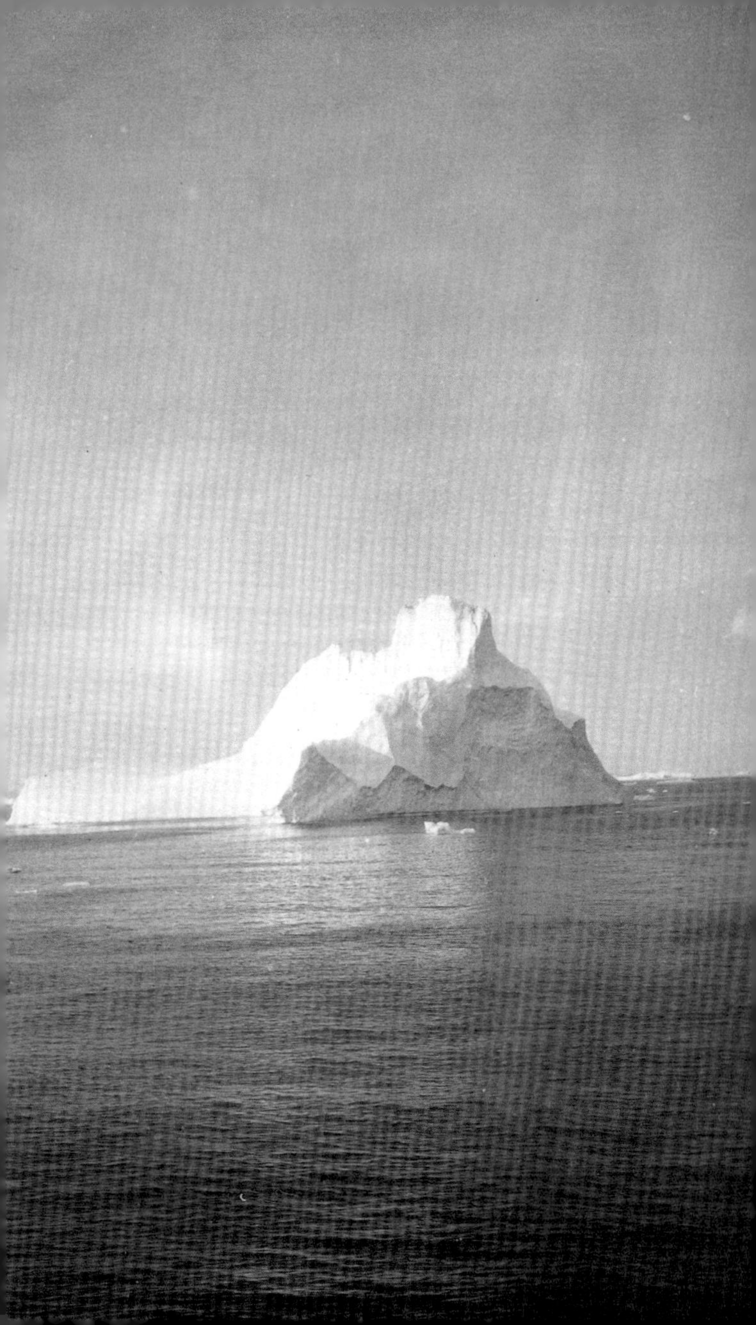

he marks out a thin arch of land in the foreground, offering us a proscenium from which to lift off into the flow of deep time, and by 1930, Harris was lifting off, the Arctic further revealing and confirming his path. As in the Ward, he moves through the space as an outsider, an observer more than a participant.

Harris has positioned viewers on the upper deck of the *S.S. Beothic*, watching forward through the rigging and over the funnel across calm open water towards a hump of rounded shoreline, a sharp mountain peak beyond. That mountain rests backlit, embraced by a bright clean aura, while a thin layer of cloud hovers about its base, exaggerating its height. The mountain is close to a perfect equilateral triangle, its silhouette reminiscent of the Great Pyramid of Giza, resembling the perfection of order and balance Harris was looking for, and intentionally constructing in his imagery—yet here it stands before him, offered to him complete (*see page 60*). It is grand and monumental and silent, yet seeming to hum with a hidden ethereal energy, rising up beyond the subtle curve of the horizon. That is what he was searching for, and a vision Canadians would come to embrace: the sublime and transcendent idea of the (Canadian) north that could hover above terrestrial realities, move outside of history, suggest a blank slate of possibility—and a convenient space of erasure.

Left: **Lawren S. Harris, Iceberg in Davis Strait, Eastern Arctic (1930)**

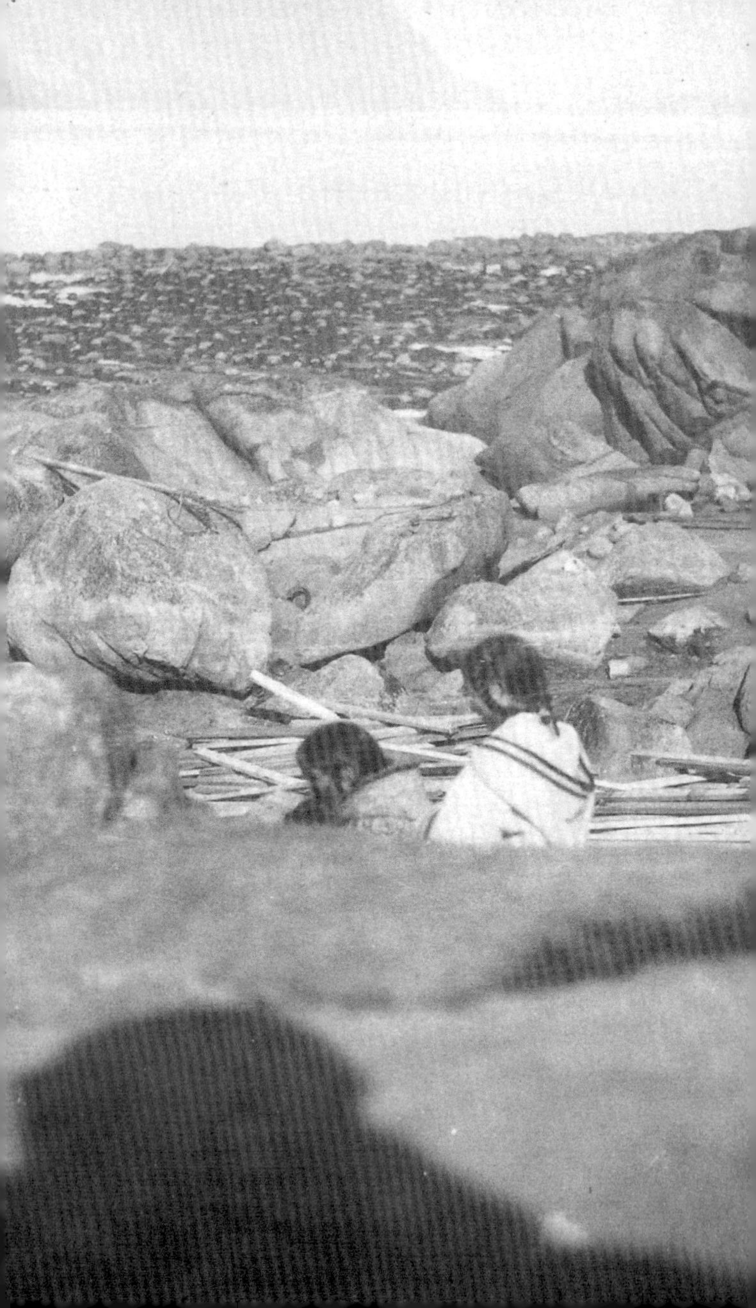

In a sense, Inuit of my generation have lived in both the ice age and the space age. The modern world arrived slowly in some places in the world, and quickly in others. But in the Arctic, it appeared in a single generation. Like everyone I grew up with, I have seen ancient traditions give way to southern habits.

— SHEILA WATT-CLOUTIER, *THE RIGHT TO BE COLD* (2015) [ix]

Left: Lawren S. Harris, Inuit Children at Pangnirtung, Baffin Island, Eastern Arctic (1930)

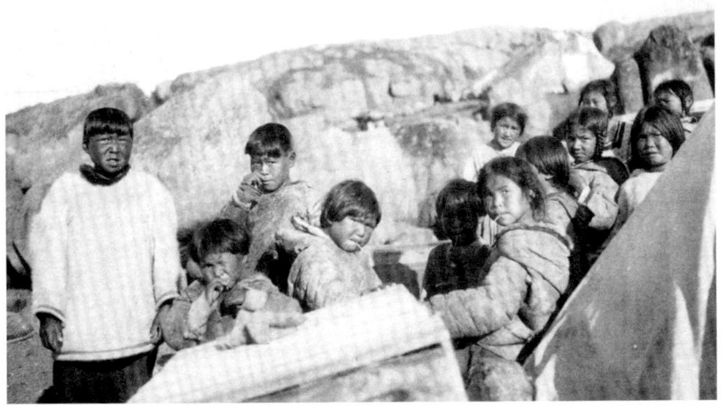

Lawren S. Harris, Inuit Children at Pangnirtung, Baffin Island, Eastern Arctic (1930)

The Arctic is rarely still and silent; it is in constant motion, both subtle and catastrophic in scale. It is noisy, calling back to you, at you, constantly. In winter the sounds are sharp and harsh, while the summer throbs with bugs and birds, sea and wind. There is a constant interaction between the body and the environment, a steady call and response best captured in the intimate embrace of two Inuk throat singers, their heavy contrapuntal breathing, punctuated by whines, cries, whimpers and screams—pleading, angry, angelic, embodying all time and space, channeling the voices of ancestors, in all forms. It is a performance of acclamation, of bold presence that demands attention, always moving forward, accumulating, engulfed in ever expanding time.

Harris's North, the North of his paintings, is monumental and mute, purely an idea, but a powerful idea that has stuck firm in the bedrock of a dominant Southern, settler sense of national self. Yet his Arctic photographs, reference material and snapshots, evince another reality. The men on the ship, with their rugged features revealing their European heritage and confident masculinity (of men in charge). The heavy iron ship churning, then drifting, then anchored, dwarfed by the slow crawl of Baffin Island's Kaparoqtalik Glacier near Bylot Island, a massive paw stretching out to dip into Pond Inlet (*see pages 76–77*). And that cluster of Inuit children at Pangnirtung, on Baffin Island's north shore: watchful, curious, suspicious, as the crew from the *S.S. Beothic* unload supplies and equipment, construction materials. They have come to stay.

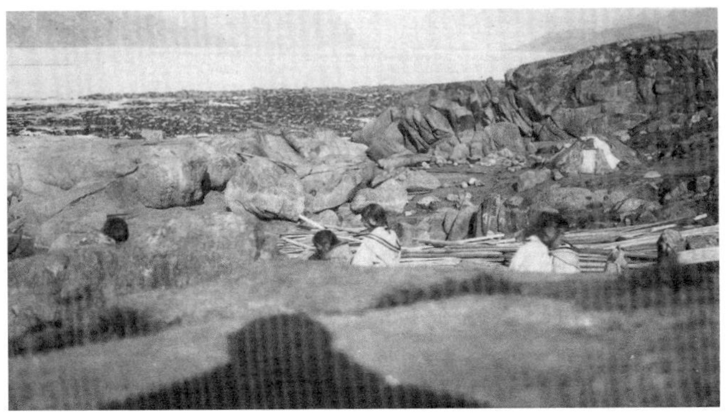

Lawren S. Harris, Inuit Children at Pangnirtung, Baffin Island, Eastern Arctic (1930)

The white man has introduced many new things that have added greatly to the comfort and pleasure of the Eskimos. Instead of spending the long hours listening to each other recount the endless details of all the daily incidents, the Eskimos may now listen to their own, or their neighbour's, phonographs, or even the radio at the Police and trading posts... The Canadian people may have no misgivings as to the manner in which the situation is being handled by Government authorities.

— DR. FREDERICK G. BANTING, *WITH THE ARCTIC PATROL* (1930)[x]

A simple life lived
On the sacred land was no more

The psalm book now replaced
The sacred songs of shamans

The Lord's Prayer now ruled
Over the haunting chant of revival

— ALOOTOOK IPELLIE, "IT WAS NOT 'JAJAI-JA-JIIJAAA ANYMORE —BUT 'AMEN'" (CIRCA 1920)[xi]

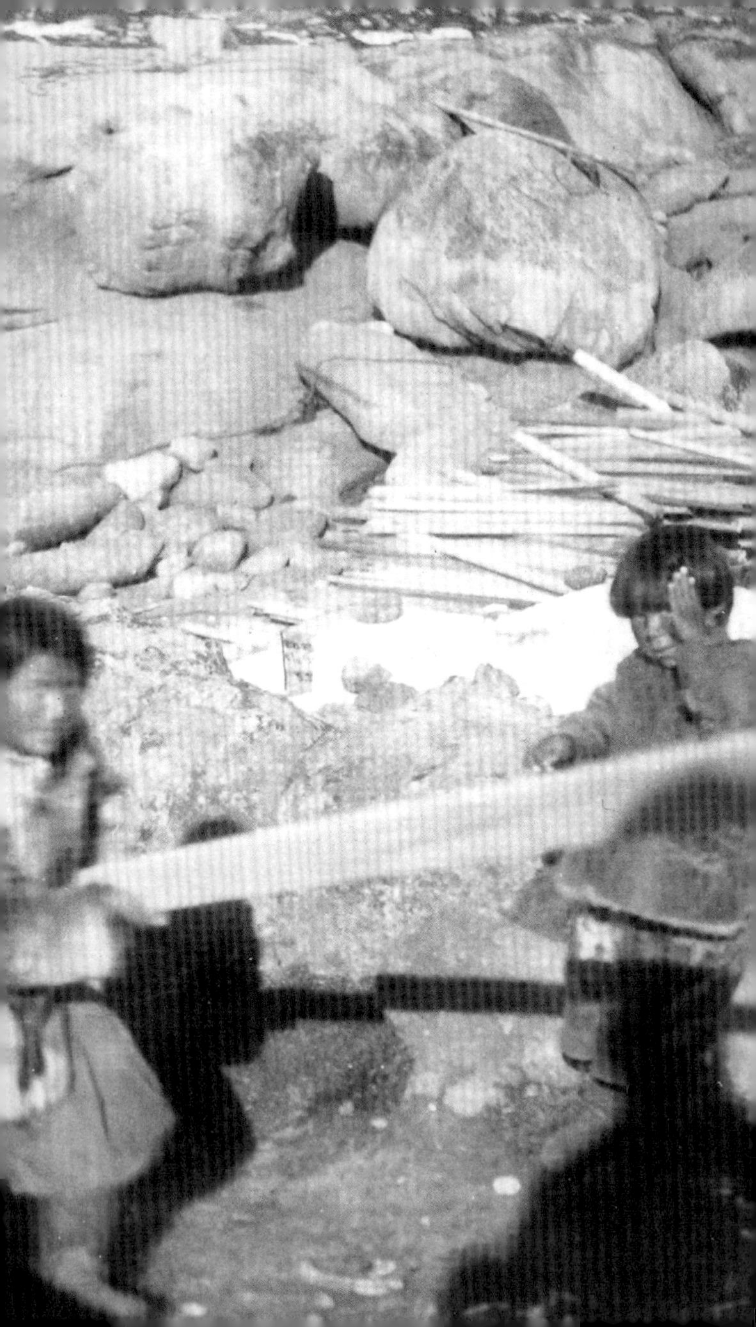

In 1930, the external forces that had been felt for generations by Indigenous people across the globe are just gaining momentum for the Inuit. Under the umbrella of the Canadian state, they will be forced into settlements, exposed to tuberculosis and a residential school system already imposed on southern First Nations and Métis peoples. They will be separated, brought south for treatment and education, and most will never return home. They will come to fight to retain their independence in this changing world, conscious of the fate of Harris's ship's namesake, the Beothuk peoples of Newfoundland, who were exterminated and declared extinct in 1829 with the death of Shanawdithit. And so Inuit voices continue resilient and resurgent.

Left: Lawren S. Harris, Inuit Children at Pangnirtung, Baffin Island, Eastern Arctic (1930)

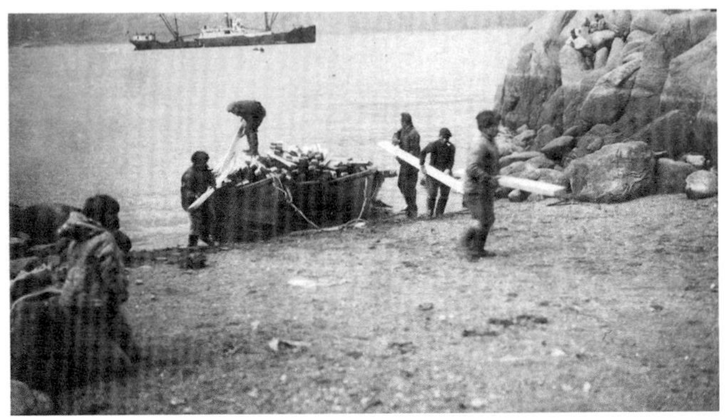

Lawren S. Harris, Unloading Supplies at Pangnirtung, Baffin Island, Eastern Arctic (1930)

It's very important that we keep our culture alive and well today, and that means accepting what it is to be Inuk today, and you know what, a lot of me today is hurting. A lot. I don't want to see people being abused and I'm sick of it. I'm mad, I'm yelling about that, I'm yelling about being sexually abused, I'm yelling about all the pain that people are having to go though, I'm yelling about all of this stuff. I think when it comes to who I am, I also feel like I'm yelling about the land, the experience of the Nuna [land] and the peace on it. The peace—the most deepest, perfect, amazing peace I've ever felt in my whole entire life and the whole root of who I am.

— TANYA TAGAQ, *VICE* [xii]

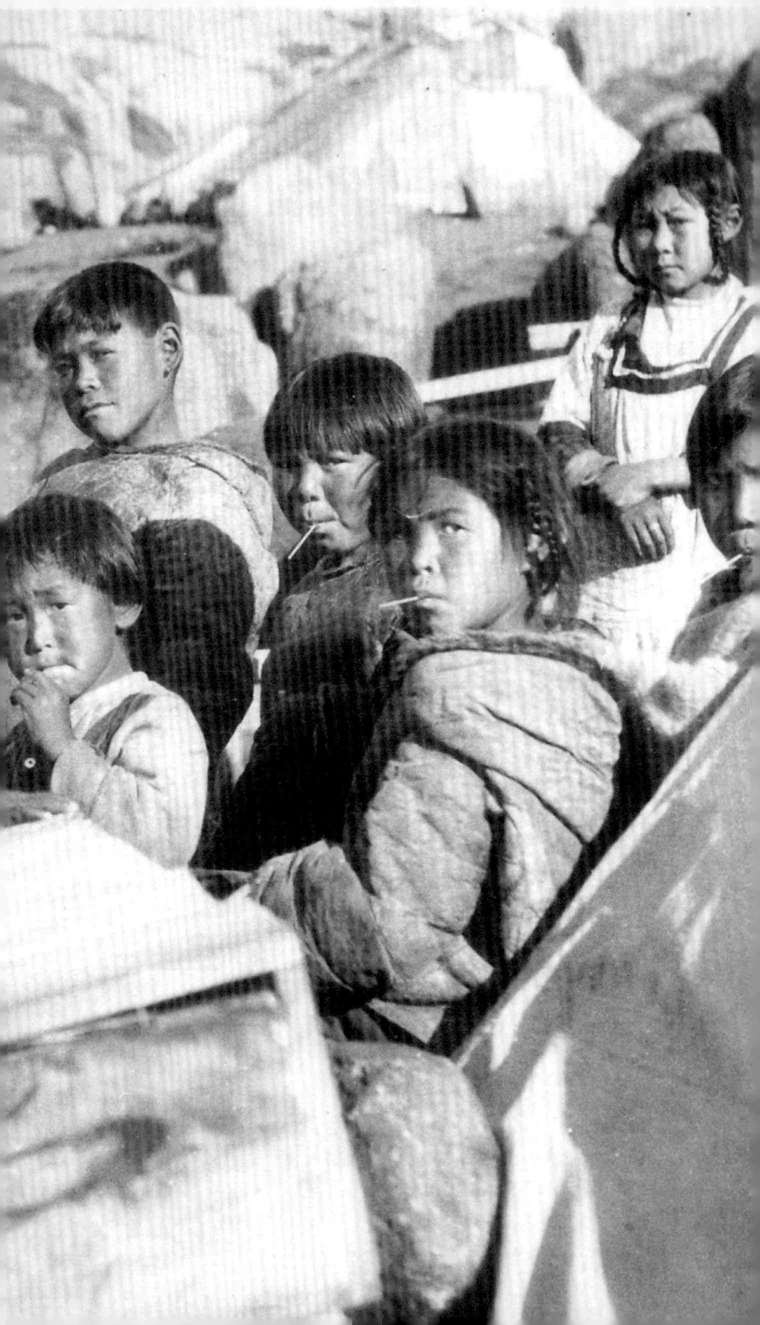

The children in Harris's photographs are of Tagaq's grandparents' generation, born of, and shaped by, their environment, who would come of age during a time of forced transition to settlements, carrying imbibed and inherited knowledge, through teachings and reincarnation, the profound memories of their past selves, knowledge unattainable by Harris and his traveling companions. Like so many before and after, they would bring preconceived ideas of this place, projecting onto this place, and the Inuit would suffer for this. You can see the skepticism in the faces of these children. They recall Goss's photographs of the Ward, unable to reflect dialogue or interaction between observer and observed, the invisible photographer distant as the children stare back (both in Pangnirtung and the Ward), evident only by a shadow cast over a rock in one image (*see page 68*). In a pair of Harris's photos, the children are huddled behind stacked crates and a thin white cotton tent, the boys withdrawing, the girls standing firm; one in particular, the thin stick of a gifted lollypop protruding from her clenched lips, appears quizzical, and then sternly defiant (or perhaps it is the other way around, as this narrative is shaped by how the images are sequenced). That defiance would continue as outsiders' values are relentlessly imposed, blanketing Inuit traditions and values that inform an undeniably contemporary people.

Left: **Lawren S. Harris, Inuit Children at Pangnirtung, Baffin Island, Eastern Arctic (1930)**

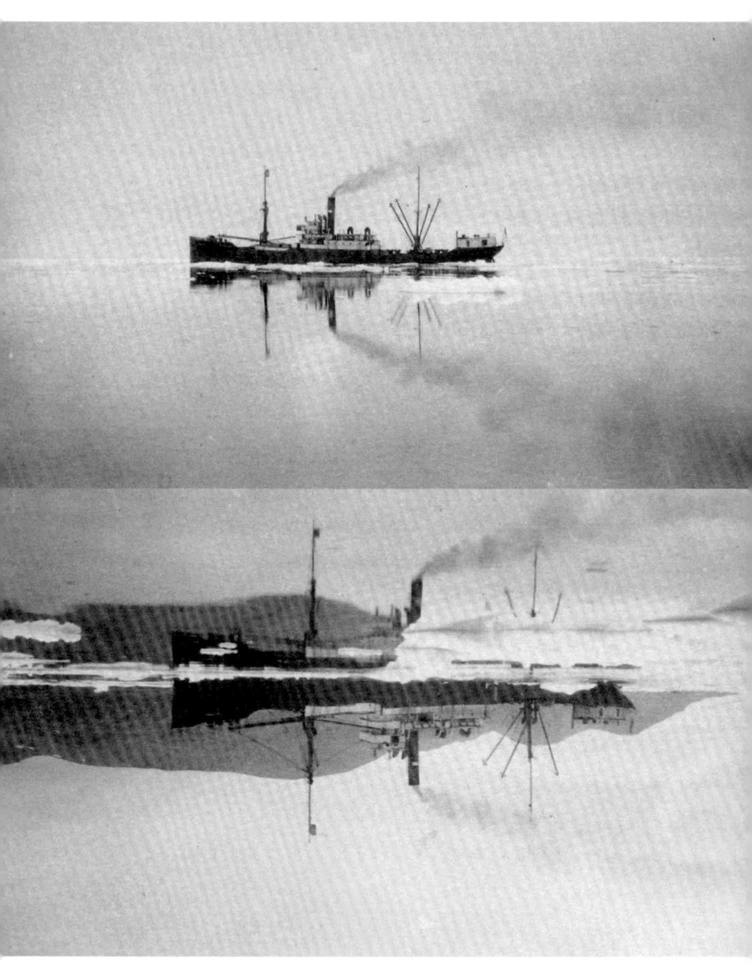

Lawren S. Harris, Four Views of the S.S. Beothic, Eastern Arctic (1930)

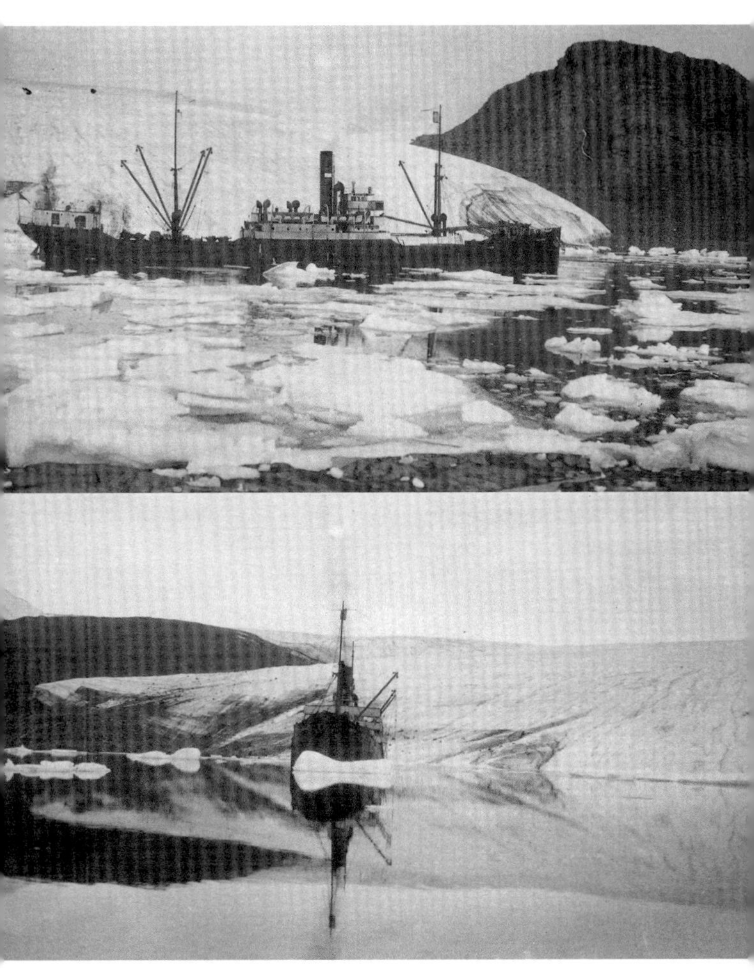

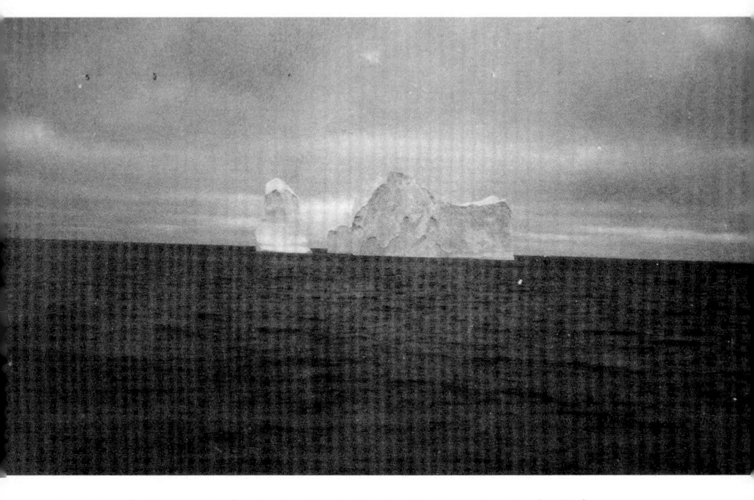

Lawren S. Harris, Icebergs in Davis Strait, Eastern Arctic (1930)

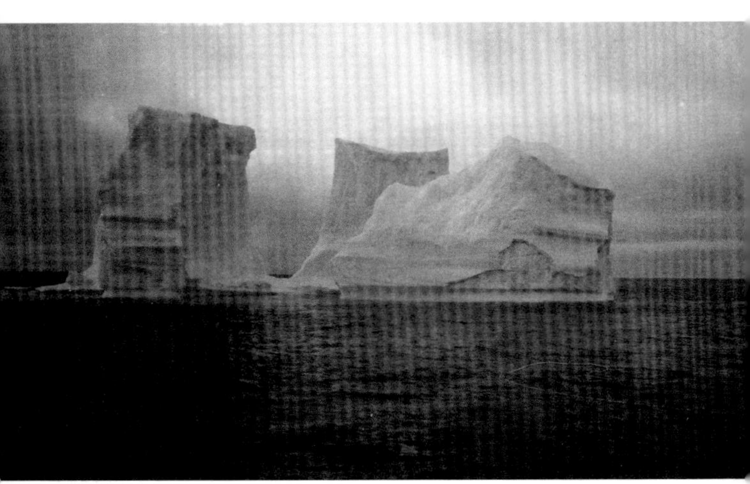

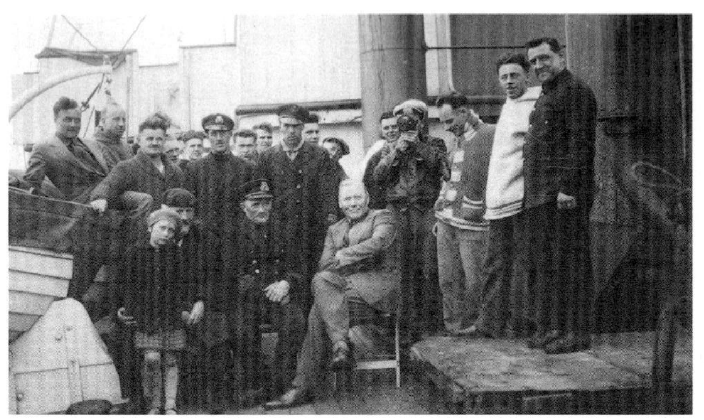

Lawren S. Harris, Crew of the S.S. Beothic, Eastern Arctic (1930)

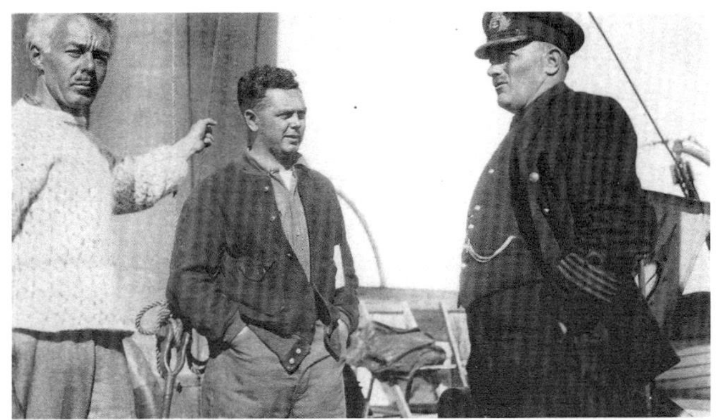

Unknown photographer, Lawren S. Harris with on board S.S. Beothic, Eastern Arctic (1930)

Next: Lawren S. Harris, Inuit Family and Summer Tent at Pangnirtung, Baffin Island, Eastern Arctic (1930)

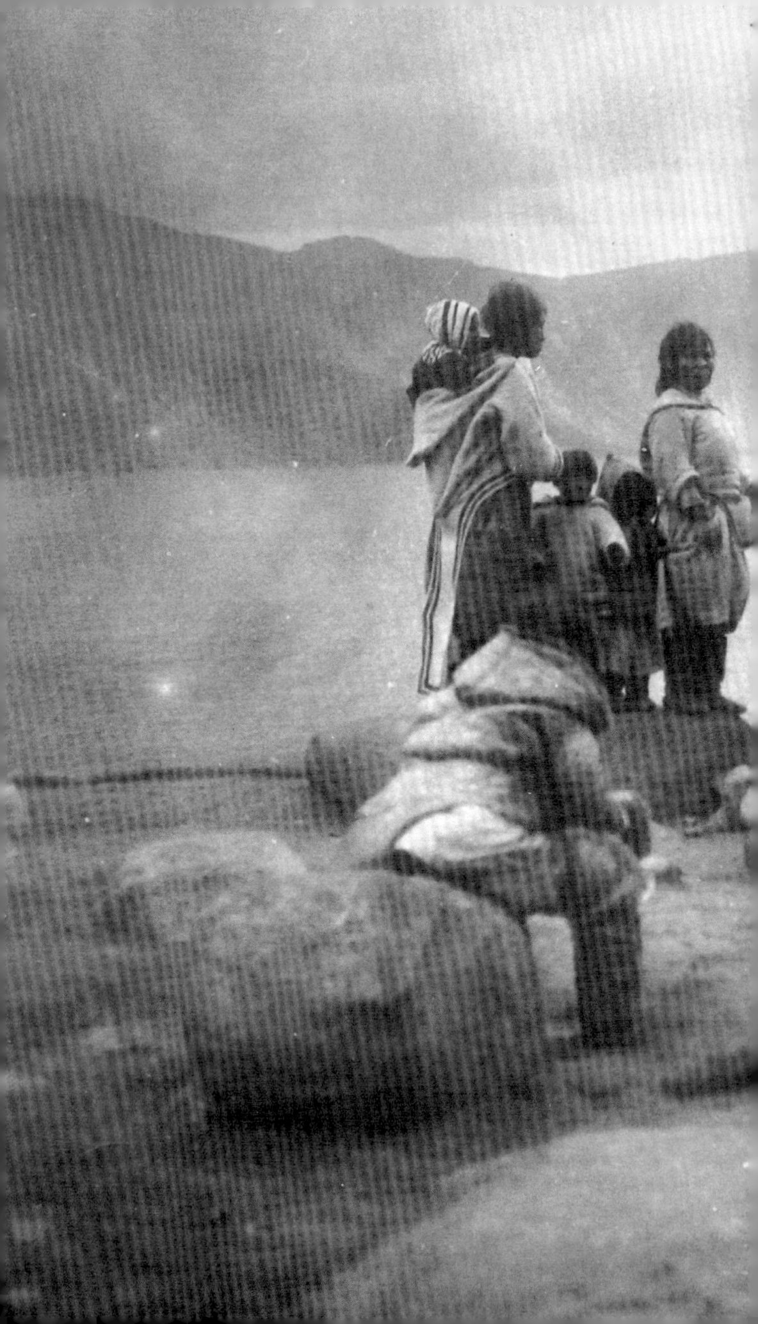

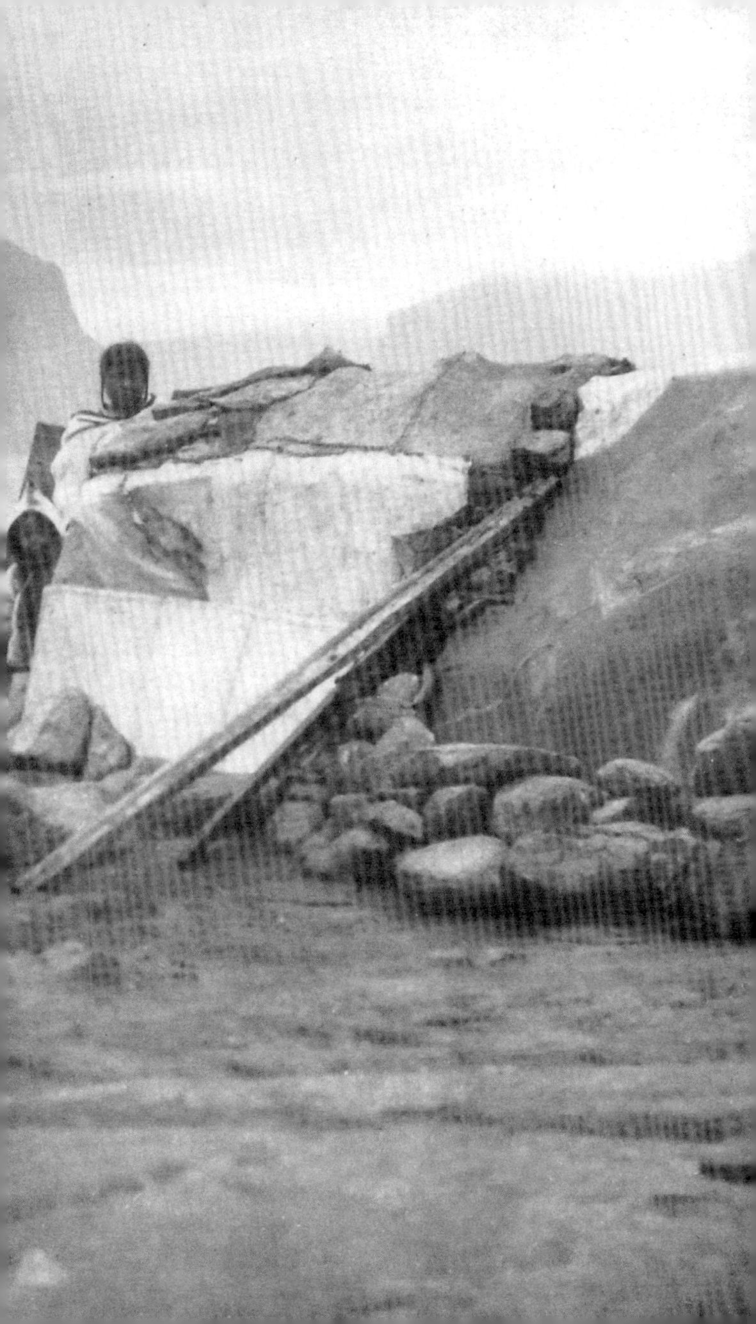

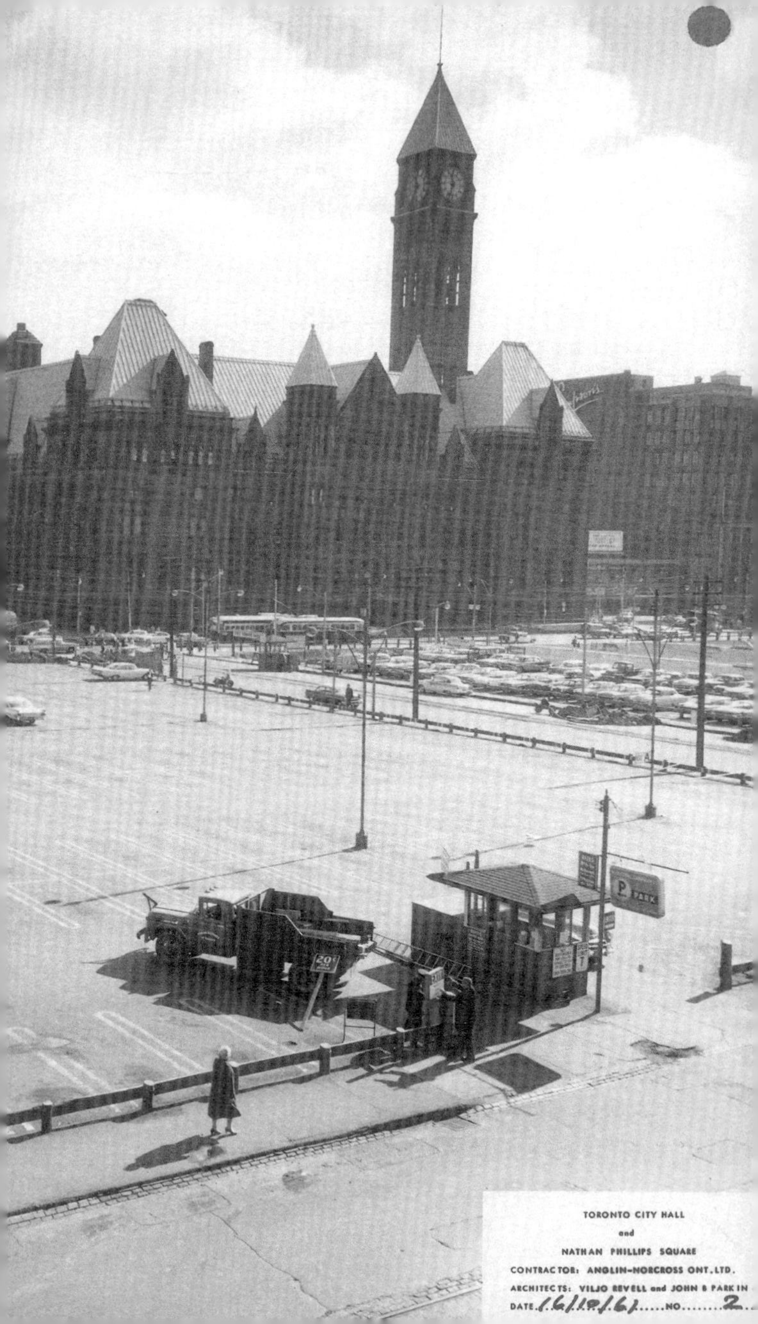
PARK
TORONTO CITY HALL
and
NATHAN PHILLIPS SQUARE
CONTRACTOR: ANGLIN-NORCROSS ONT. LTD.
ARCHITECTS: VILJO REVELL and JOHN B PARKIN
DATE 16/10/61 NO 2

Part 3
In the City

In 1936, having left Toronto, first for New Hampshire and then New Mexico, Lawren Harris produced a painting that most Torontonians would be hard pressed not to consider without being reminded of the new City Hall and Nathan Phillips Square. Titled *Poise* (*see page 86*), the work consists of two curving architectonic forms towering over a central sphere, deeply resonant of Finnish architect Viljo Revell's modernist vision anchoring the city centre adjacent to Toronto architect Edward James Lennox's older Romanesque city hall that still stands at Bay and Queen, facing the original Eaton's flagship store. Before Eaton's it was Simpson's, and then The Bay (then called the Hudson's Bay Company, founded in 1670 and named after Henry Hudson, who was cast adrift by his disgruntled crew while searching for the Northwest Passage to Cathay). Even today they sell the striped HBC blankets and an assortment of Canadiana souvenirs, including Inuit carvings and Inukshuks, Canada's newest and latest international symbol (replacing the generic totem pole, wildlife, and, to a degree, the paintings of Tom Thomson, the Group of Seven and Emily Carr—although all of these iconic symbols are often mixed together). That nationalist narrative of land and appropriated indigeneity claimed by Harris's generation has remained robust, at times irrepressible and irresistible, both inside and outside of Canada.

Left: Panda Associates Architectural Photography, Parking Lot at Chestnut and Albert looking South East (October 16, 1961)

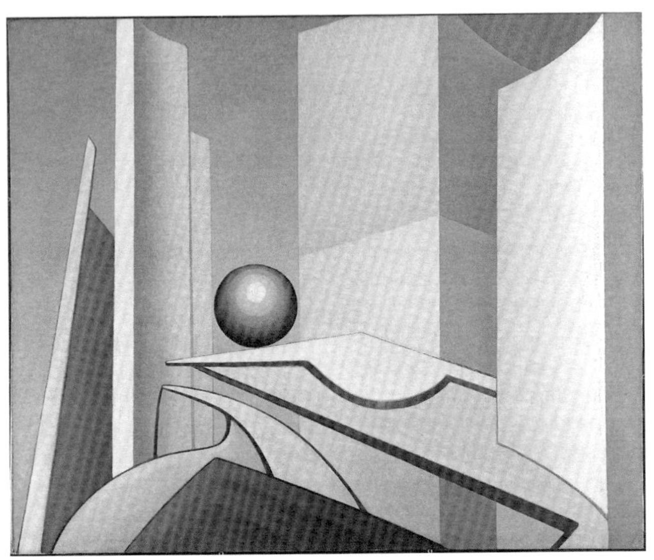

Lawren S. Harris, *Poise* (1936), oil on canvas

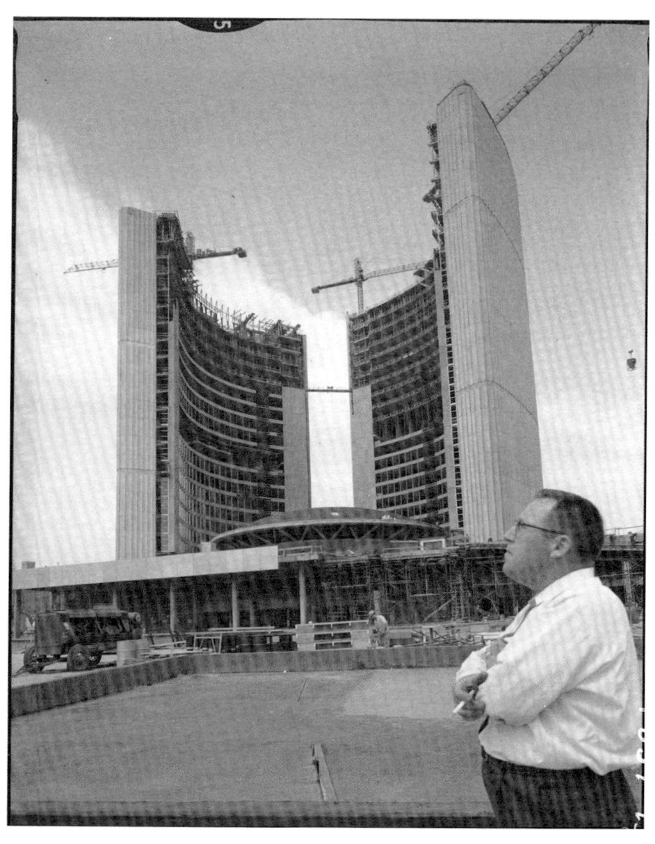

Construction of New City Hall, International Union of Operating Engineers (1964)

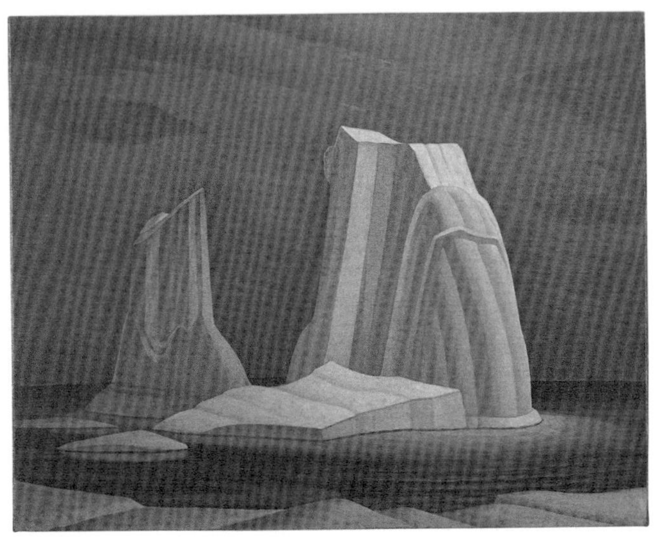

Lawren S. Harris, *Icebergs, Davis Strait* (1930), oil on canvas

In the foreground of *Icebergs, Davis Strait*, Harris has once again added what feels like the lip of a stage, drawing the Leviathan up to the shore, and I take it all in as if the scene has been laid out in front of me to possess. It has become iconic, and in its intensity and clarity remains a boldly modern idea; yet like many modern ideas, it is both powerful and problematic. Not widely known outside of Canada, Harris's paintings have become national icons at home, symbols of a resilient conception of a country that has historically identified deeply with the land (primarily, however, only as idea and resource). In the drive to establish an identity tied to this land, to articulate a sense of belonging in a particular place, imbued (like the *terroir* of wine or cheese) with the essential characteristics of a distinct terrain, much is left out and many voices remain silenced. Harris's classic, modern paintings can be easily read as an idealized articulation of this drive to new fundamentals, a new story set within the emergence of Canada as a confident, independent nation following World War One.[xiii] The sense of permanence and clarity of his modern vision that Harris offered in his paintings have resonated on a deeper level than the work of many of his contemporaries (both within and outside Canada). The country's dominant mythology would be a burden to his later, more universal (and frustrated) transcendental ambitions, and can be considered baggage that still accompanies the reception of his northern landscapes of the 1920s and 1930s.

Harris's northern landscapes were for the dominant settler culture of Southern Canada, not the Inuit. They can be irresistible and strangely comforting, an ideal contrast to our current climate of uncertainty. Indeed, modernism can be appealing for its succinctness and the suggestion of a deep

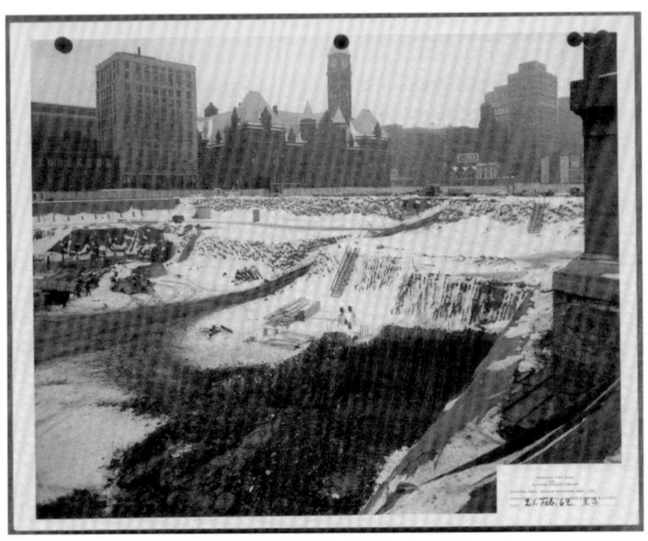

Panda Associates Architectural Photography, Preparing Foundation of New City Hall and Nathan Phillips Square (February 8, 1962)

sense of programmatic focus and knowledge, representing the things an individual, nation, and perhaps even a species hopes for. But such confidence can easily shift towards arrogance. It can be dangerous to assume we know where we stand, and to interpret an image of a moment as evidence of the whole truth. The iconic power of Harris's northern landscape paintings as emblems of Canada is potentially their greatest contemporary weakness, as their stark, still emptiness lingers at odds with the reality of a diversely peopled place and culture living in a vulnerable and besieged environment. Moreover, "whiteness" as purity, order, solidity, and cleansing light may have sounded progressive when articulated within a particular context (like the term "virility" used by many period reviewers of Harris and the Group of Seven), but has become deeply and increasingly problematic. In Canada, one cannot encounter a Harris piece as just a painting, positioned outside the shadow of history and national narrative. Whiteness is the elephant in the room, the pale leviathan always looming beneath the surface.

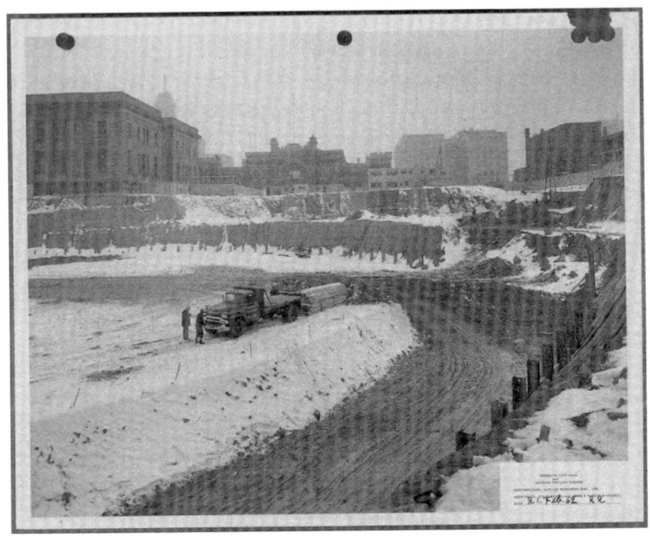

Panda Associates Architectural Photography, Preparing Foundation of New City Hall and Nathan Phillips Square (February 8, 1962)

Here again I confront whiteness, snow and ice, but not in the far North or in a classic Harris painting. I am hovering over an open pit, a deep excavation on the ground Goss, James and Harris once traversed. In 1960, from Queen to Louisa, Chestnut to Bay, a rectangle of expropriated land obliterated streets (sections of Elizabeth, Chestnut, Albert and Louisa), and much of the city's original Chinatown was pushed west, following the Jewish community that fled earlier along Dundas to Spadina. Scant traces remain of the once bustling heart of the Chinese community: a few restaurants, family associations, and an Ontario Heritage plaque in memory of Jean (Toy Jin) Lumb, who led the fight to preserve Chinatown. A Canadian, born in Nanaimo, British Columbia in 1919, she lost her citizenship when she married Doyle Lumb in Toronto, a man born in China whose family had paid the Head Tax to emigrate here. Together they opened the Kwong Chow Restaurant, one of the four famous establishments that raised the community's profile in the city and made Chinatown a popular destination. She would become a citizenship court judge, a leader in the business community, and eventually an Officer of the Order of Canada. The little parkette at Elizabeth and Foster Place where her plaque was recently unveiled is adjacent to the former site of the Hong Luck Kung Fu Association, founded partly because young Chinese men were regularly assaulted in the city. It became a gathering place for martial arts and lion dancers, and also, along with other family associations, a place to borrow funds when no Toronto bank would give loans to Chinese businesses.

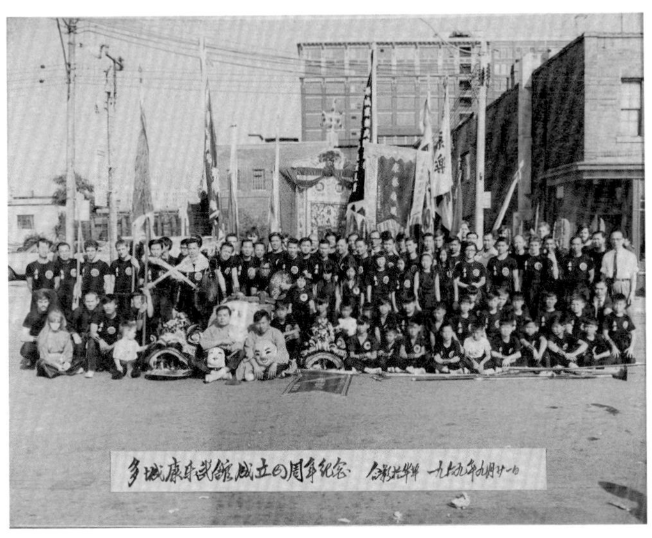

Unknown photographer, Hong Luck Kung Fu Association, Elizabeth Street (1969)

In a fading photo, the Hong Luck Kung Fu associates gather outside on the site of the parkette, young and old, a giant lion head resting on the curb, their many banners flapping in the summer breeze. Towering over them in the distance is the red-brick Eaton's warehouse, soon to fall victim to the wrecking ball to make way for the Eaton Centre that will occupy all the land of Timothy Eaton's warehouses and factories, and many of the dilapidated homes pictured by Goss. For several years, following the expropriation, there was a blank space, a parking lot and cleared blocks, leveled land waiting, like the square of earth now dormant behind hoardings where the British Methodist Episcopal Church once stood at 94 Chestnut, one of the oldest Black churches in the city. Sacred ground (*see pages 128–131 and back cover*). And then in 1961, the excavations began, into the heart of the Ward.

February 1962, fifty years since I stood in those frozen yards, buried in snow, confronted by the faces of those evicted. The city looks cold, *another grey day in town*, the excavation site blanketed with new snow, the sky heavy with more. The towers of the old City Hall and Canada Life Building loom in the distant, the latter's illuminated tower flashing its weather forecast, bright white light for the coming storm. There's the Eaton Manufacturing Building, and the Casino Burlesque Theatre faces us from across Queen at Bay, while streetcars shudder past, still in the rust and yellow of the Blackburn Cab company. There is a mild, cruel irony to the fact that a professional architectural photography firm called Panda was commissioned to document the construction of a structure that obliterated the original Chinatown.

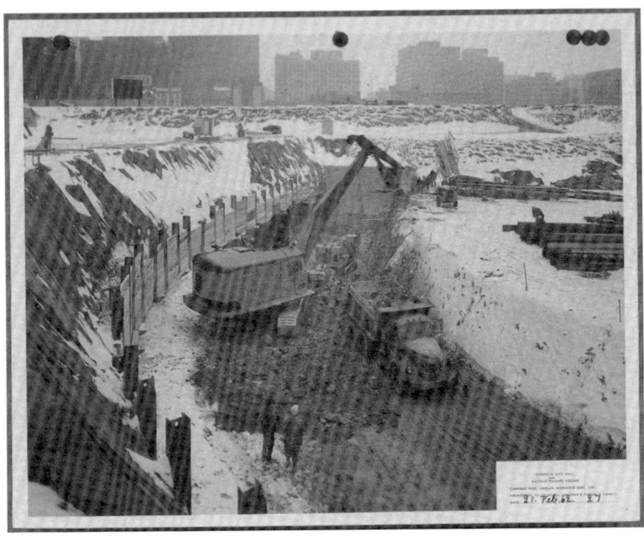

Panda Associates Architectural Photography, Preparing Foundation of New City Hall and Nathan Phillips Square (February 8, 1962)

I gaze down at the trucks and earthmovers carving out curves for Revell's two towers, readying the ground for the I-beams to support their foundations. Later, they will construct the core, the round concrete pillar that supports the flying saucer council chamber the towers embrace. I am watching them as they, unaware, construct Harris's vision from *Poise*, the stark space of the new City Hall, foreshadowed by Harris's vision of an empty cool modern landscape, devoid of a human presence. The towers will rise, and in 1965 they will be hailed as a catalytic symbol ushering in a modern era of progressive ambition and a new international spirit in the city, a distinct break from the old Orange-order *Toronto the Good*. During the evening's opening ceremonies, the buildings are bathed in light, glowing, while spotlights project a perfect triangular halo that hovers in air above the square (*see pages 110–111*). It is as if those divergent paths from the early twentieth century—Toronto's urban renewal and Harris's aspirations for transformation and transcendence—have fused on the burying grounds of the Ward, rising from the erasure of forgotten lives.

Harris left the city in 1934. He would often visit, but never again live here, spending his final decades, from 1940 to 1970, in Vancouver. His art and ideas would help to shape dominant concepts of Canada, the *Great White North*, empty and open, ready for development, free from history. But it is precisely through this supposedly progressive vision that the complexity and diverse narratives have largely become erased, written over. Canada as a model multi-cultural state emerged only in recent decades, although prefigured and influenced by John Murray Gibbon's *Canadian Mosaic* of 1938,[xiv] but this is often projected as a new phenomenon, ignoring the deep history of Indigenous peoples and a truly diverse and complicated web of

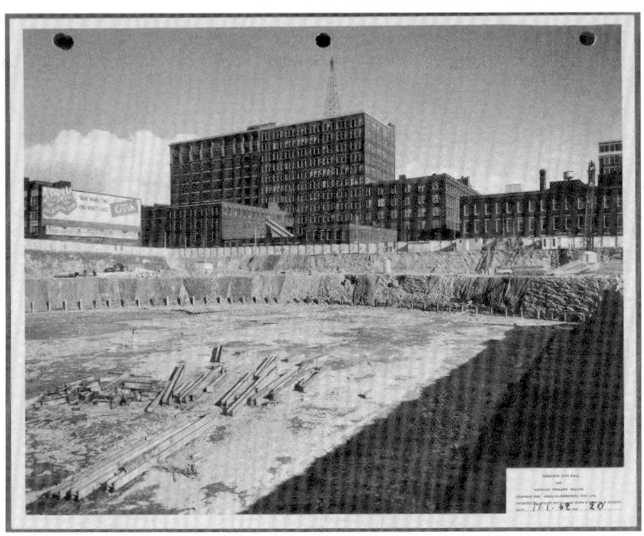

Panda Associates Architectural Photography, Site of New City Hall and Nathan Phillips Square (November 6, 1961)

multi-origin settler cultures, complicated by the growing presence of formerly colonized and displaced peoples, of enslaved peoples. Idle No More, Black Lives Matter: these movements are potent reminders that so much remains unresolved, so much that cannot be fixed by regularly trotting out red mittens embossed with maple leaves, building Inukshuks on Toronto's lakeshore, or fantasizing about pure untouched wilderness in an idyllic northland when the Arctic sea ice is melting, the Rocky Mountain glaciers that inspired Harris are vanishing, and high temperatures and drought have engulfed Fort McMurray, near the tar sands region in Northern Alberta, in raging wildfires as I write this.

I return to the Ward with my daughter Claire to find the exact spot of Lawren Harris's 1911 painting of the Eaton Manufacturing Building, and Goss's photo behind Elizabeth Street, the one with the young girl alone in the long woolen coat with her mysterious book. I have placed the former on a spot southwest of the Church of the Holy Trinity, the latter in the middle of Nathan Phillips Square. I've laid the 1913 Goad Fire Insurance Map over a contemporary map of the city, and the site of Harris's painting puts us in the centre of the north end of the Eaton Centre, between the escalators, within the clerestory looking south where the massive warehouse once stood (*see page 8*). We wander down the full length of the mall, past Michael Snow's flock of Canada Geese, and then loop back to Nathan Phillips Square. With Goss's photo in hand, we maneuver to find the spot, and when we locate it, we are both startled to find ourselves amongst a crowd taking photos of family and friends clustered around the giant multi-coloured TORONTO sign that edges the skating rink. Claire holds the photo and I position her on the spot where that other young woman once stood; behind her, another girl, alone, takes multiple selfies (*see pages 100–101*).

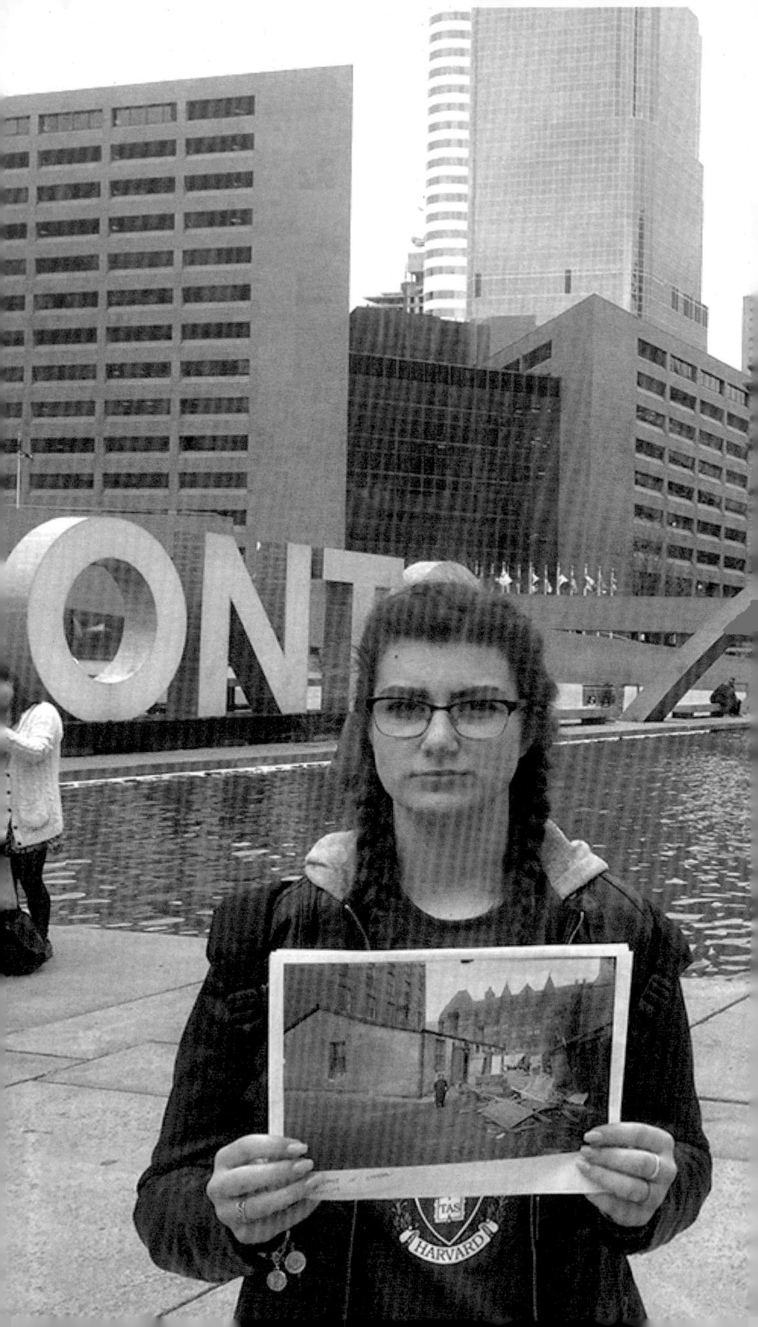
ONT
HARVARD

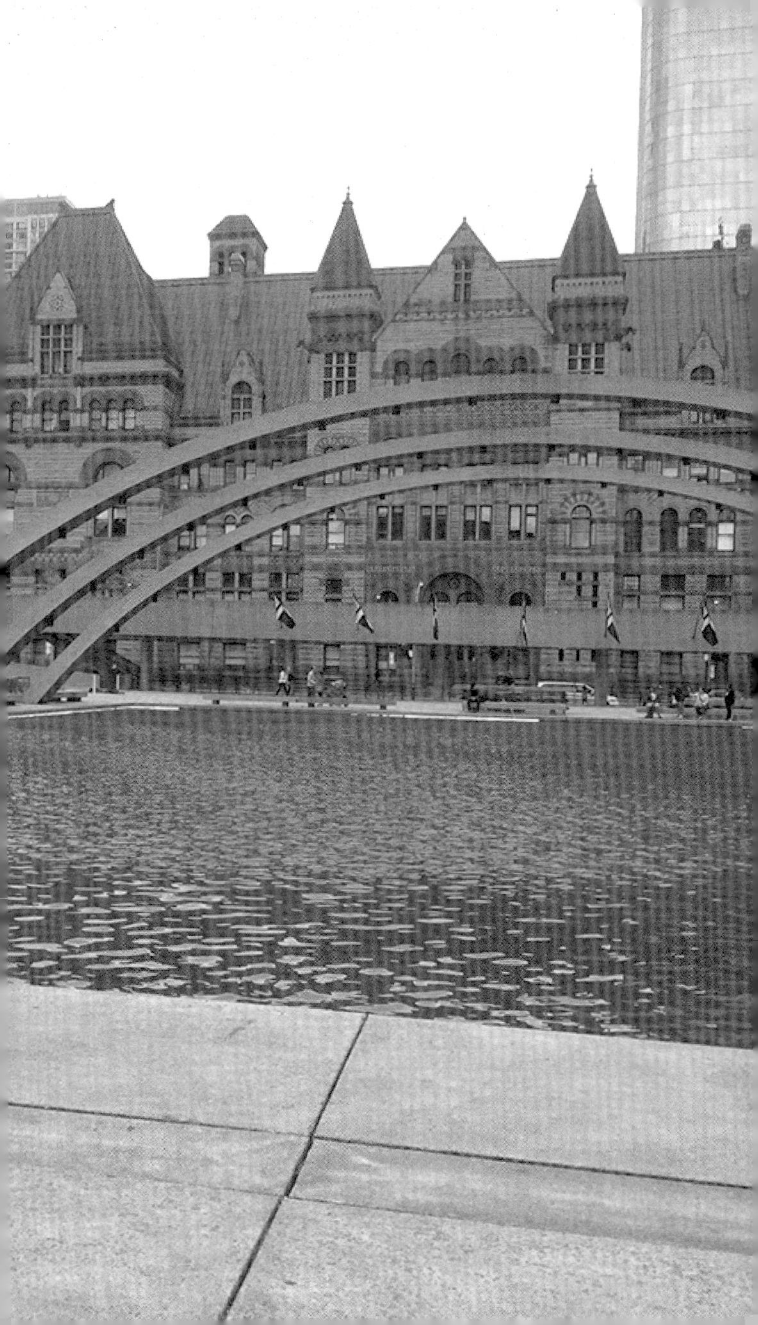

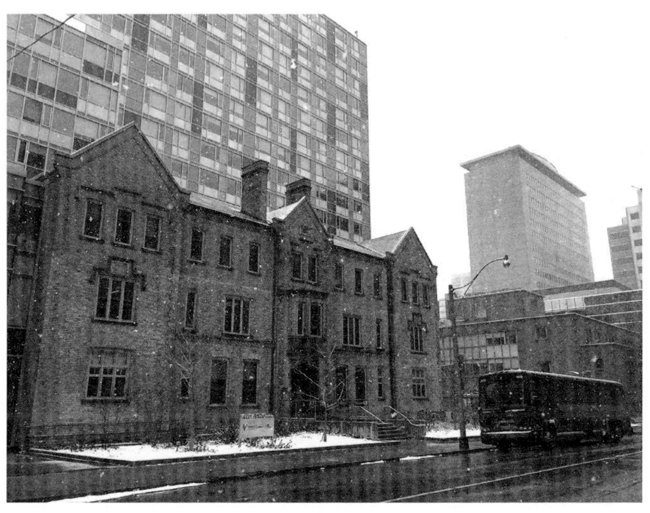

Andrew Hunter, Poorhouse (now part of YWCA Elm Street Centre), 87 Elm Street (2016)

Previous: Claire and Andrew Hunter, *Site of Arthur Goss's Rear of Elizabeth Street*, 2016

We walk back north through Nathan Phillips Square, past the city hall, up Elizabeth Street and across Dundas Street stopping on the northwest corner of Elm where we turn back and look southwest. It is spring but the temperature has dropped and there are light flurries drifting down. We are facing 87 Elm Street, architect William Thomas's elegant Victorian "poorhouse" or "house of industry" built in 1848 and based on the British model, it is now part of the YWCA complex. Looming in the distance is a grey concrete office block, the original new city hall design, rejected then repurposed for Imperial Oil. This rejection spawned the architectural competition that led to Revell's winning design. At the poorhouse, men and boys would have to break stones in the yard to earn their keep. Y'know, it was a bad time to be poor," I tell her, quoting that sad Rheostatics song.[xv] "Well, when isn't it?" she observes.

We head east on Elm so I can show her St. Georges Hall, home to the Arts and Letters Club, Harris's homebase in the Ward. We imagine him heading out, wandering the neighbourhoods, dreaming a future, troubled by what he sees around him. *All those absent bodies still haunt this place.*

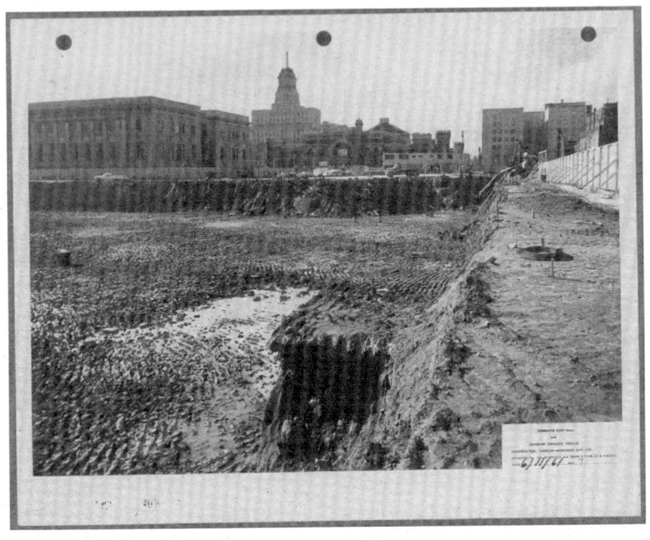

Panda Associates Architectural Photography, Site of New City Hall and Nathan Phillips Square (November 6, 1961)

...and Evening

Towards evening I walk down street
Through the crowds returning from the daily grind.
The air is stale and heavy.
Everyone is weary and hurries homeward, intent on rest.
People are occupied with themselves and salute one
another grudgingly, or not at all.
They have nothing for their fellows.
The rattle and clanging of streetcars, the roar of
heavily laden trucks, the piercing bleat of arrogant
motor horns—all discordant noises of
the street
Bespeak to them the jangle and futility of human affairs.
Facing homewards, people swarm from the daily grind.

— LAWREN HARRIS, *MORNING AND EVENING* (1922) [xvi]

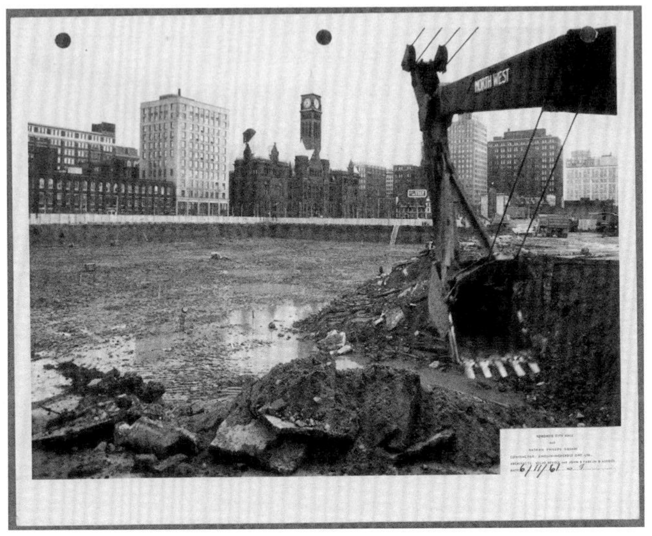

Panda Associates Architectural Photography, Site of New City Hall and Nathan Phillips Square (November 6, 1961)

Next: Panda Associates Architectural Photography, Construction of New City Hall (November 19, 1962)

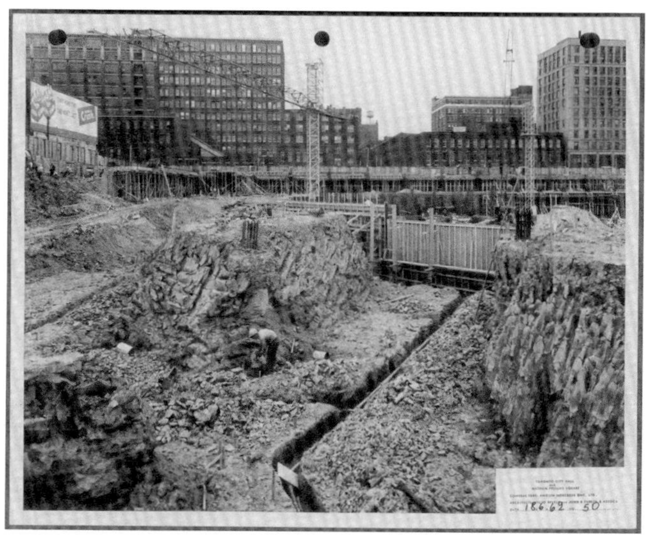

Panda Associates Architectural Photography, Preparing Foundation of New City Hall and Nathan Phillips Square (June 18, 1962)

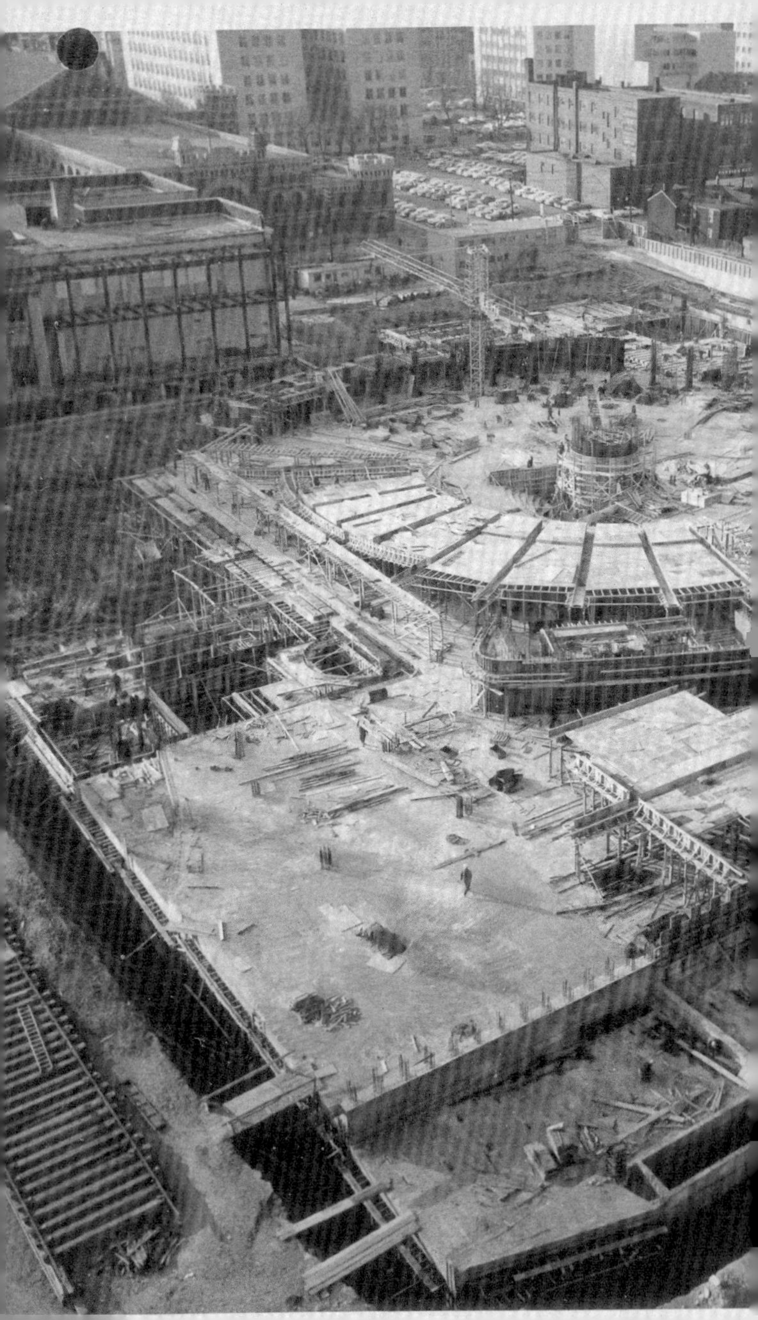

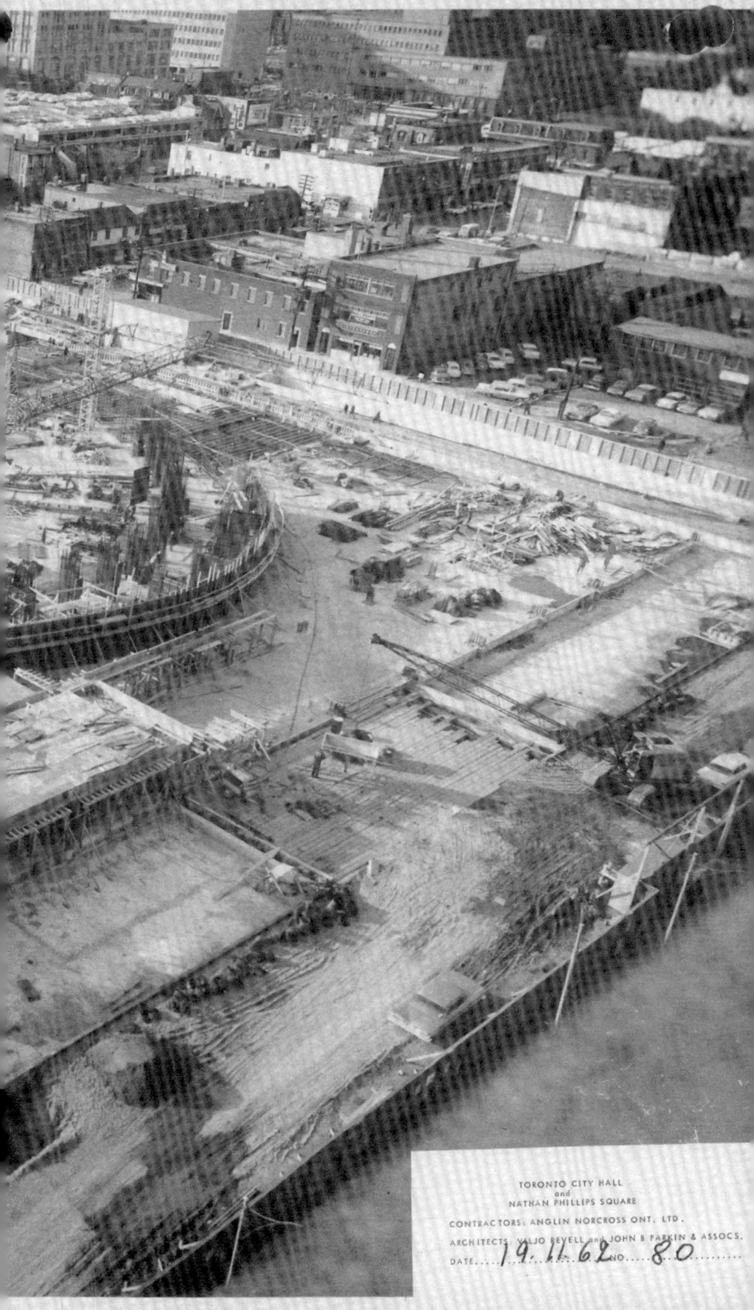
TORONTO CITY HALL
and
NATHAN PHILLIPS SQUARE
CONTRACTORS: ANGLIN NORCROSS ONT. LTD.
ARCHITECTS: VILJO REVELL and JOHN B PARKIN & ASSOCS.
DATE 19.11.62 NO. 80

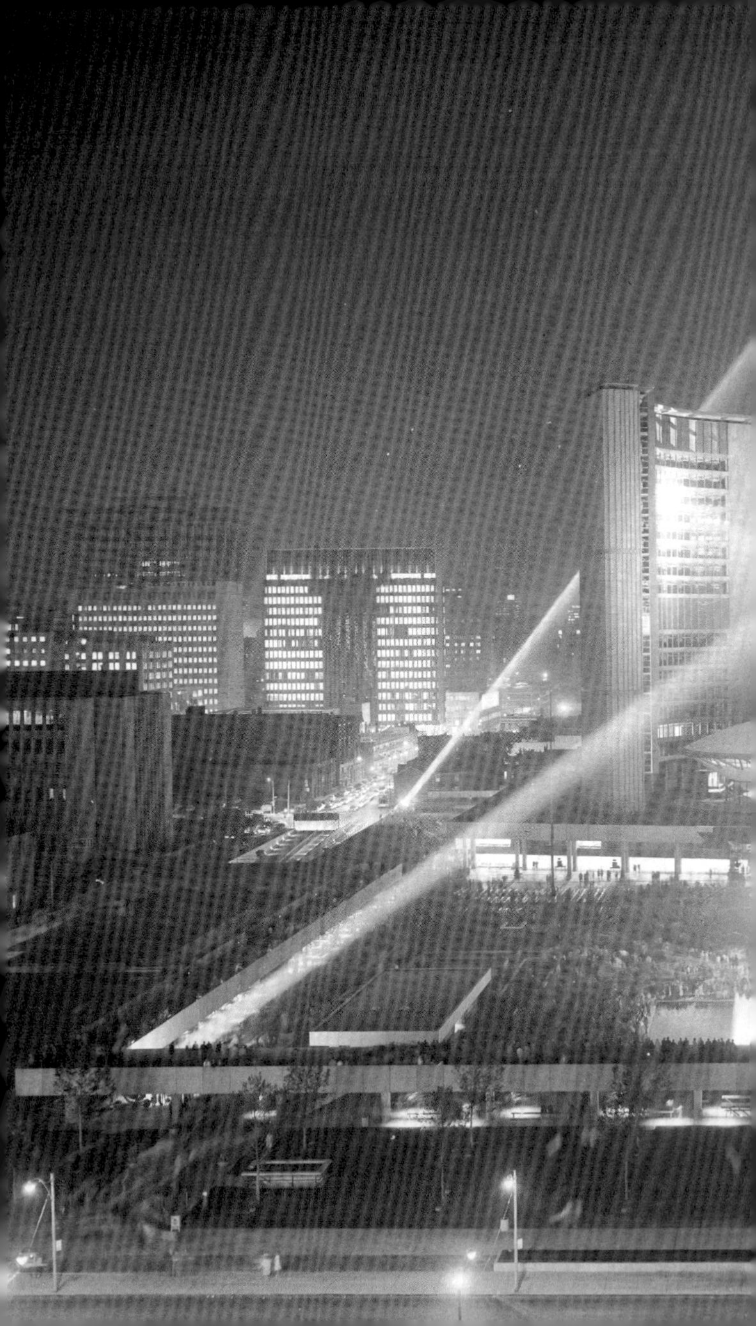

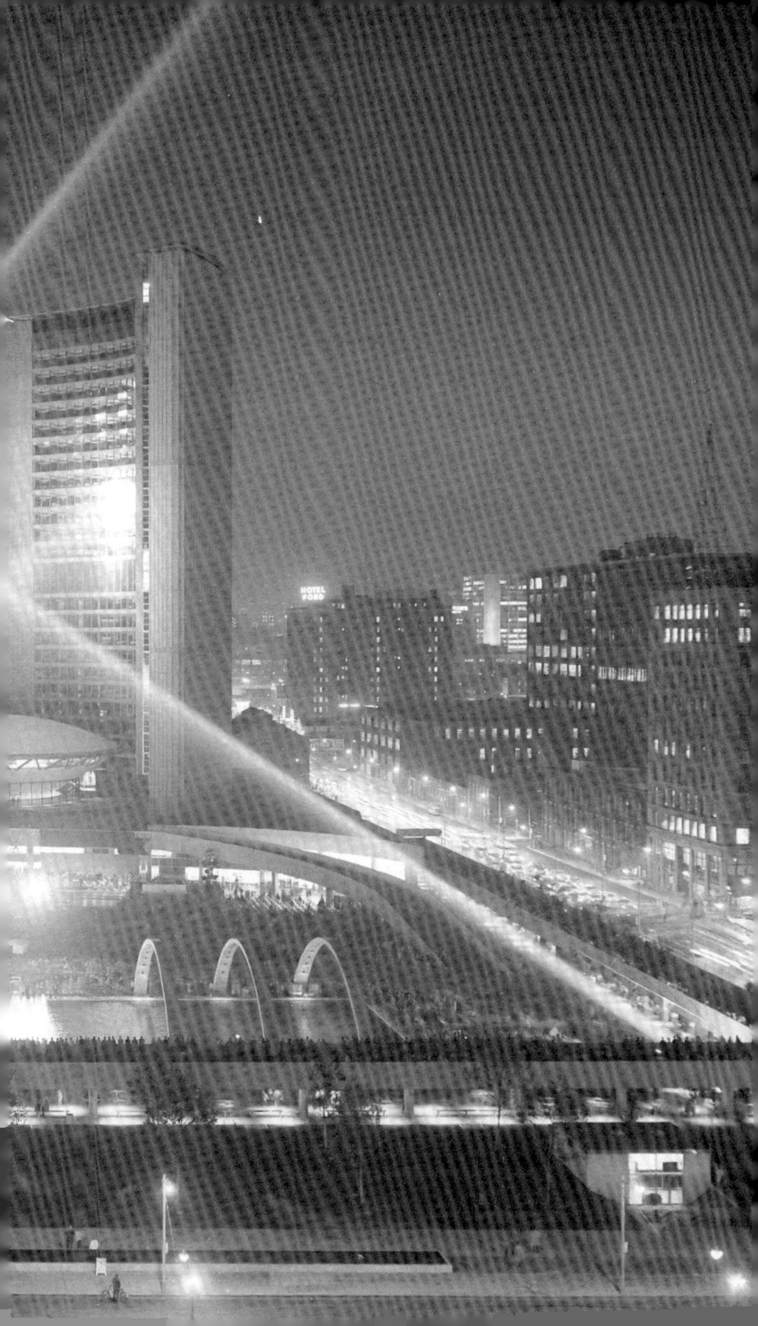
HOTEL
FORD

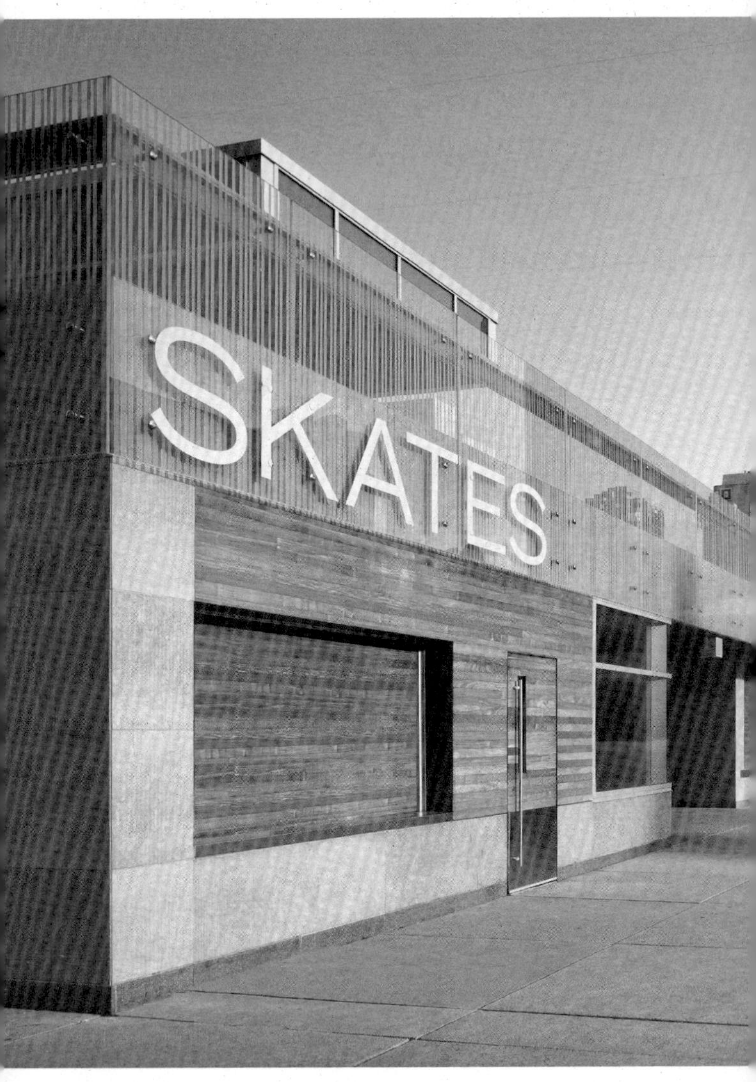

Previous: Toronto Fire Department commissioned photographer, from the series Opening week, New City Hall and Square night shots, showing lighting of New City Hall and Fireworks (September, 1965)

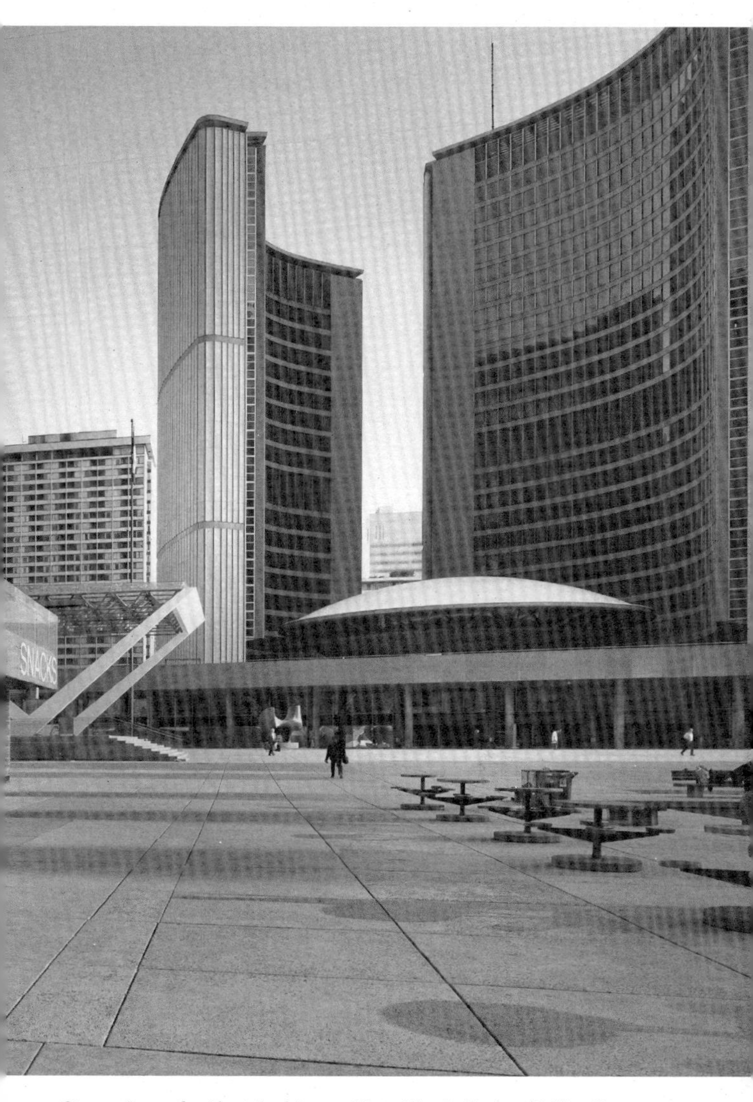

Steven Evans for Plant Architects, *Skate Shack, Nathan Phillips Square and New City Hall* (2015)

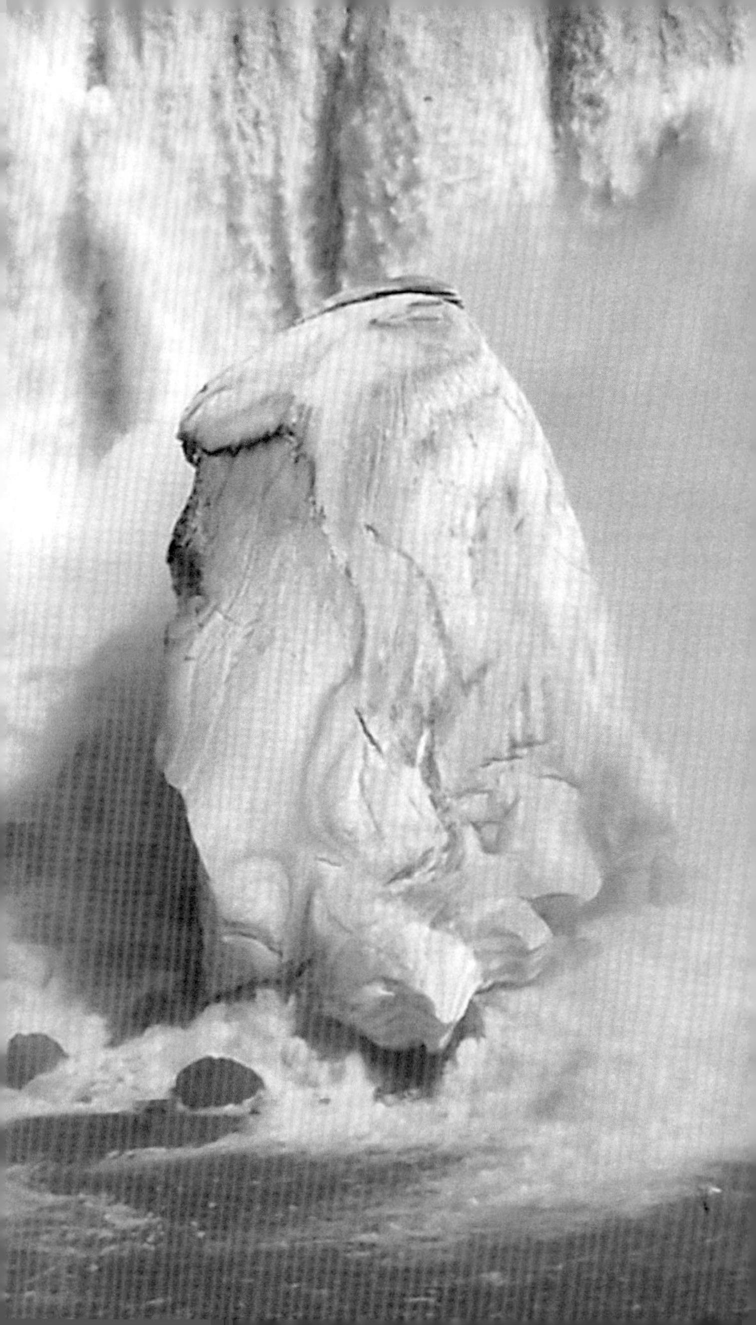

Part 4
Artists' Projects
Tin Can Forest
Anique Jordan
Nina Bunjevac
Jennifer Baichwal & Nick de Pencier

In the Ward includes reproductions of art by Toronto artists commissioned for the AGO presentation of *The Idea of North: The Paintings of Lawren Harris*. These works brought a contemporary perspective to themes of erasure and renewal, Toronto history, ideas of Canada and the North.

Left: Jennifer Baichwal & Nick de Pencier (Mercury Films), Detail of *Ice Forms at American Falls*, Niagara (2015)

Tin Can Forest (Pat Shewchuk & Marek Colek)

Seven Sermons of the Dead: A Guide to Lawren Harris's Dream (2016)

The sequence of images reproduced here compliments the animated video and curtain/altar (illustrated with mystical symbols) that appeared in the exhibition. The work narrates a fictional dream of Lawren Harris's in which he longs to transition from the earthly realities of the Ward into sublime transcendence in an imagined North. It was inspired by *The Divine Comedy* in which Dante envisions three stages of the afterlife. Tin Can Forest's animation pictures *the Ward* (Purgatorio) where (*pages 124–125*) in the initiate (Harris) sleeps and wanders, dreaming of spiritual ascent, a journey to Northern Mountains (Paradiso). For Tin Can Forest, the Ward is haunted ground infused with deep spiritual and mystical power.

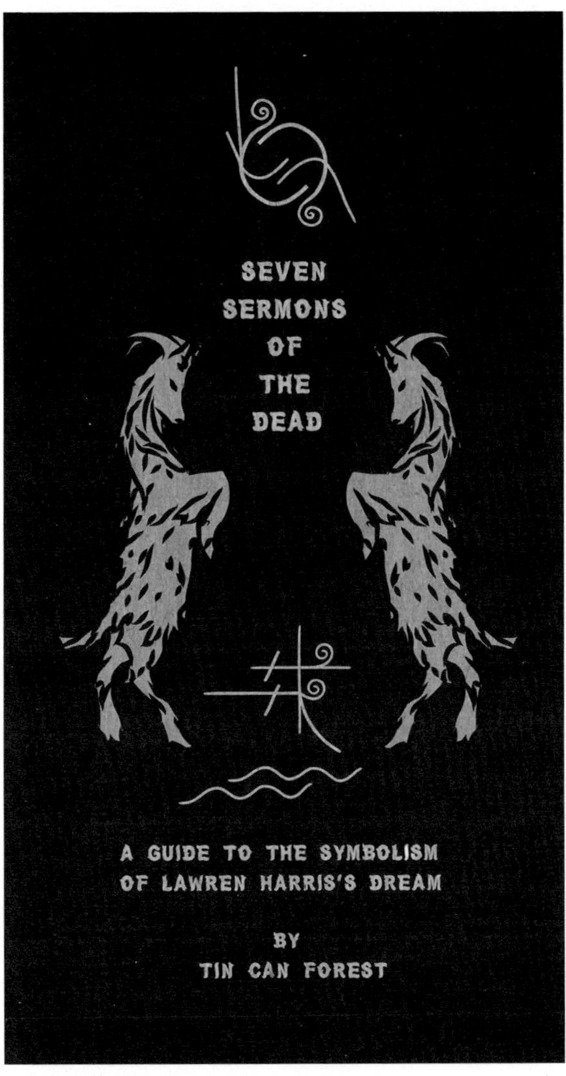

Tin Can Forest (Pat Shewchuk & Marek Colek), *Seven Sermons of the Dead* (2015–2016)

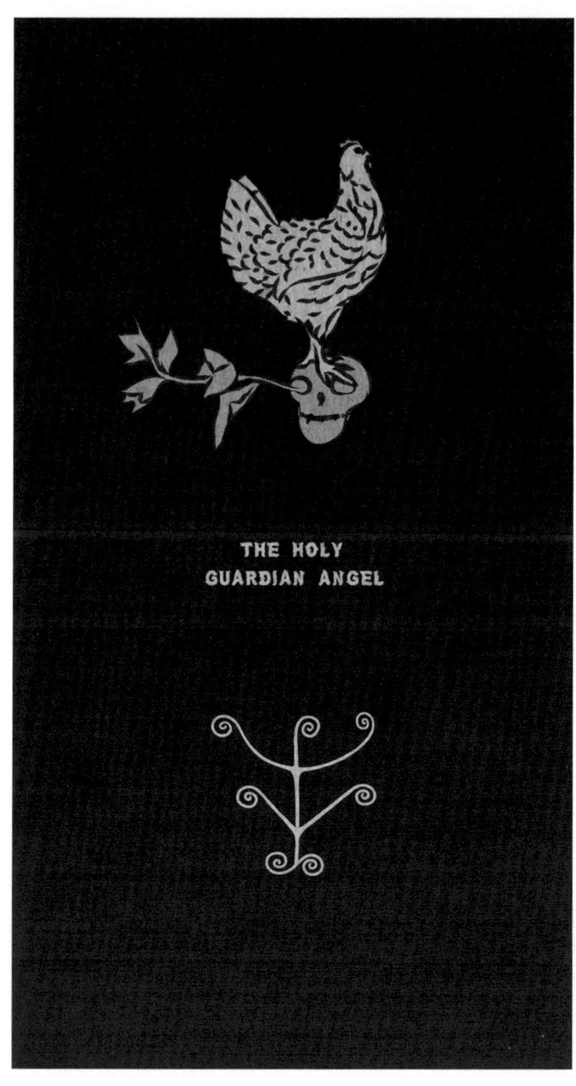
THE HOLY
GUARDIAN ANGEL

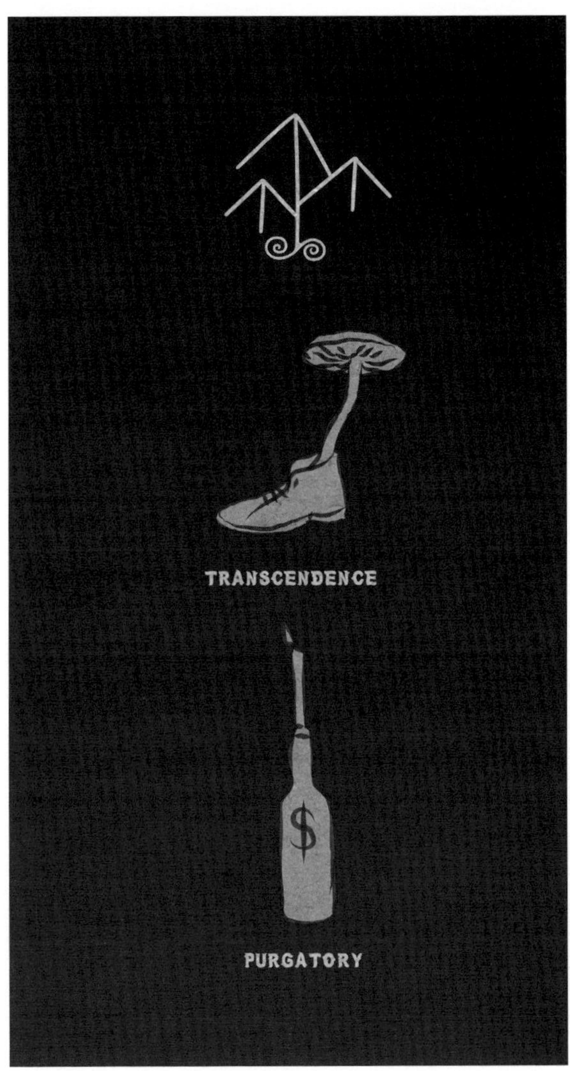
TRANSCENDENCE
$
PURGATORY

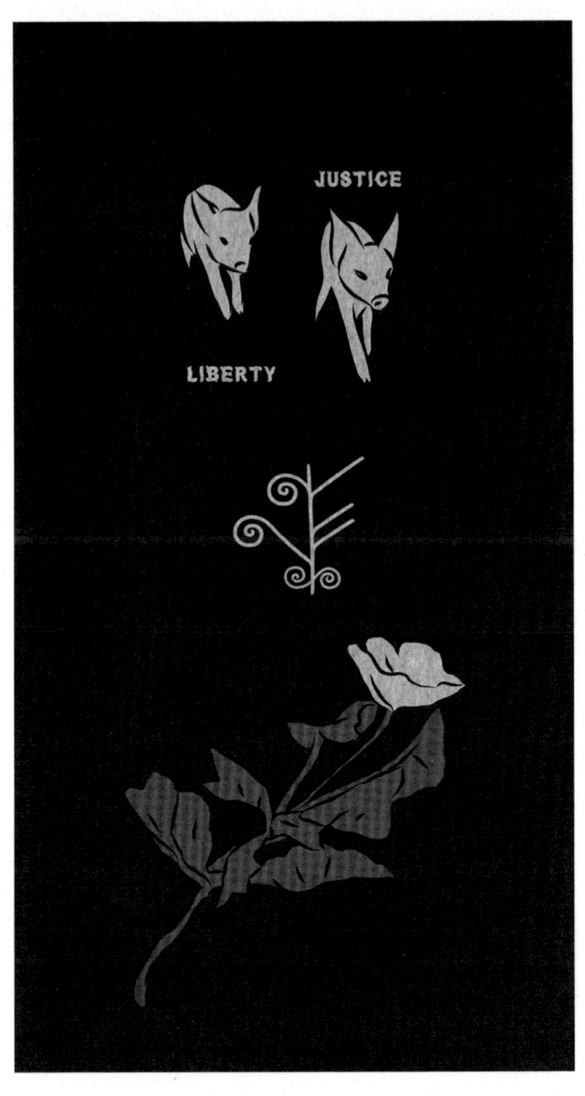
JUSTICE
LIBERTY

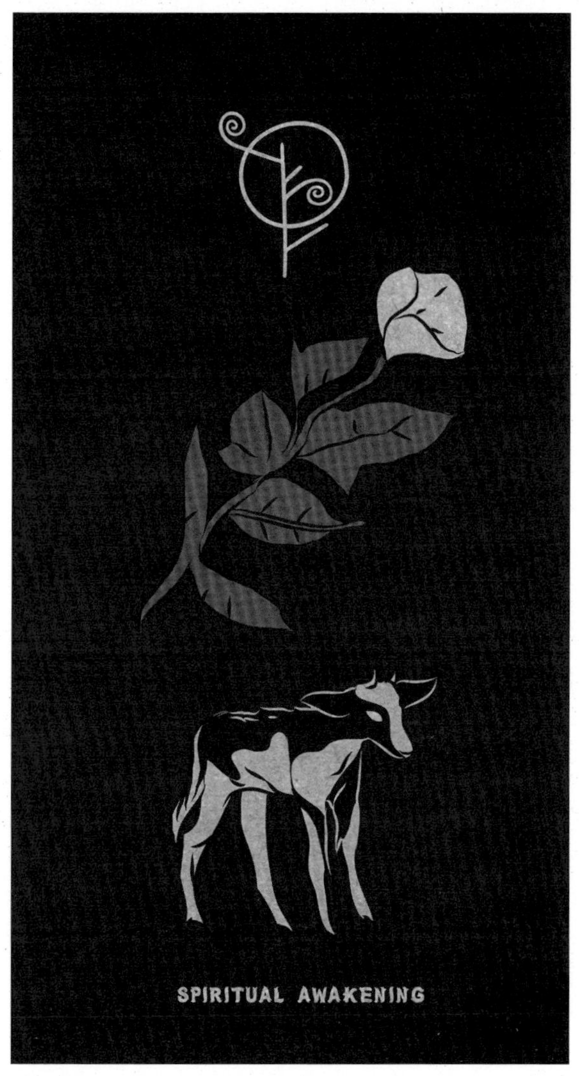
SPIRITUAL AWAKENING

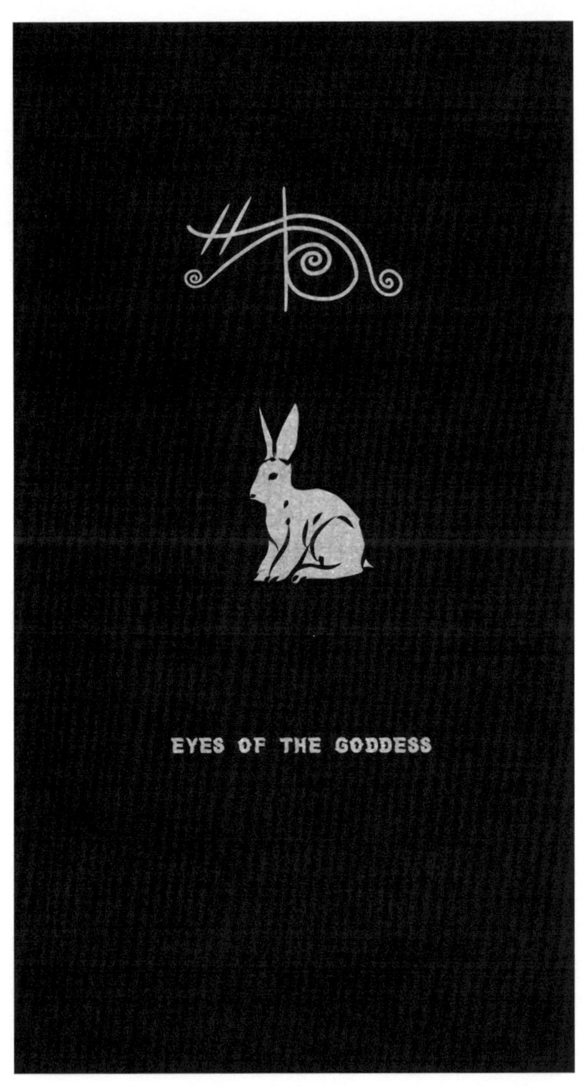
EYES OF THE GODDESS

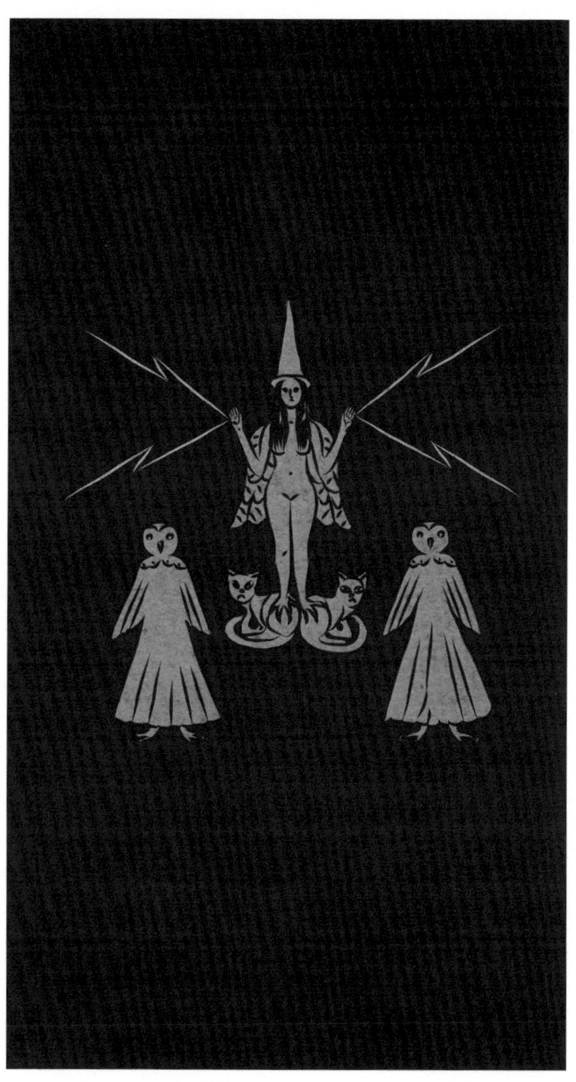

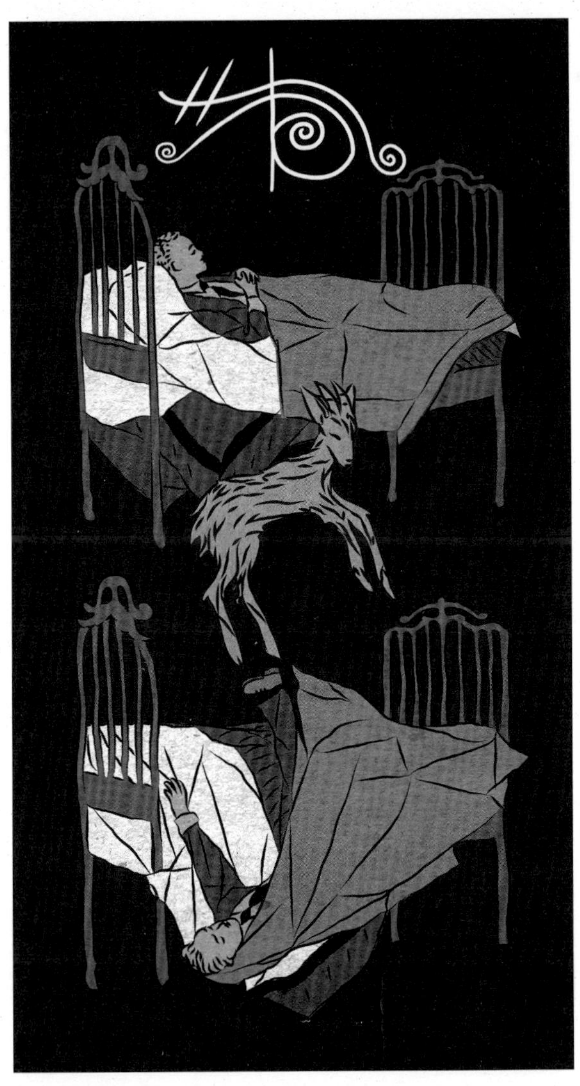

Tin Can Forest (Pat Shewchuk & Marek Colek), *Isis Unveiled; Lawren Harris's Theosophical dream; A Divine Comedy* (2015–2016)

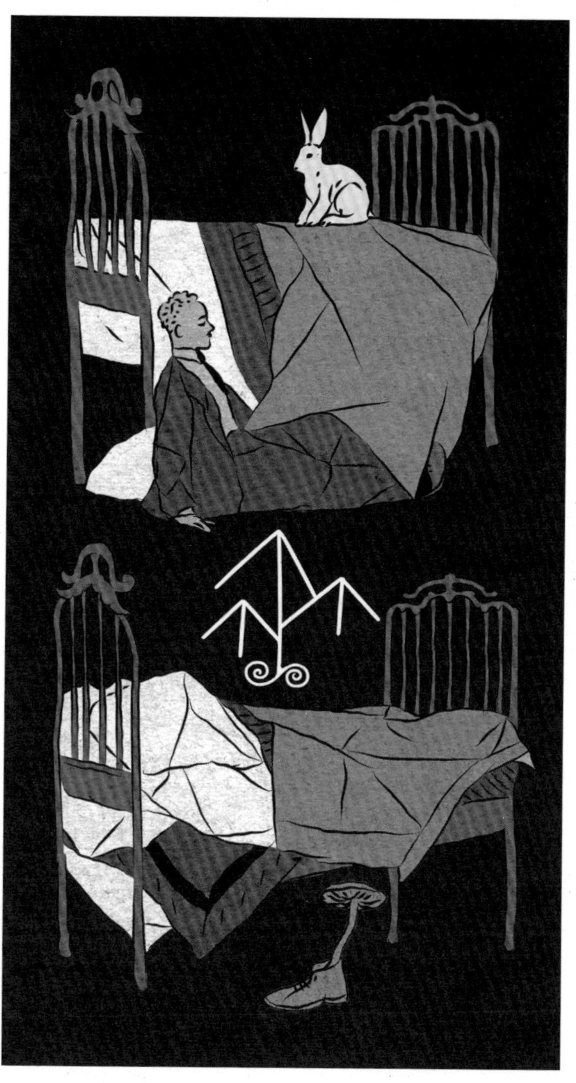

Anique Jordan

94 Chestnut at the Crossroads & *Mas' at 94 Chestnut* (2016)
Black and white reproduction of original colour images

A young Black woman in Victorian mourning dress is barred entry to a site of sacred ancestral significance to Toronto's Black community, the British Methodist Episcopal Church at 94 Chestnut Street. In the series of four images that make up the complete work, she rotates clockwise to the four cardinal points. Beneath her feet and on the wall behind her are diagrams based on West African and Haitian symbols that call the spirits to gather, be acknowledged and witness her creation of a crossroads. Two Black hands raised behind her cast a memory of recent calls to action from Black communities. *94 Chestnut Street at the Crossroads* is a powerful image of resistance against the violent systemic erasure of Black histories and bodies in Toronto. For Jordan, this woman defines a "literal crossroads with her body from which we can imagine a center point where the visible and the invisible might meet."

Jordan wishes to acknowledge the support of Petrose Tesfai, Rudy Powel, Louis March, Ato Seitu, Paster Chester Searles, Miss Milly, Gloria Clarissa, Lystra Curtis, Cheryl Seitu, Virgilia Griffith, Sandy Hudson, Danielle Smith, Aisha Bentham, Vero Diaz, Erin Howley, Angaer Arop, Alyssa Fearon, Kerri Byam, Ilana Divantman, Aisha Bentham, Charmaine Lurch, Michèle Pearson Clarke, Paul Bailey, Marsha Williams, Ella Cooper, Isa Ransome, Joanna Prescod, Daphne Fraser, Carolyn Jordan, Patrick Parson, Church of Holy Trinity.

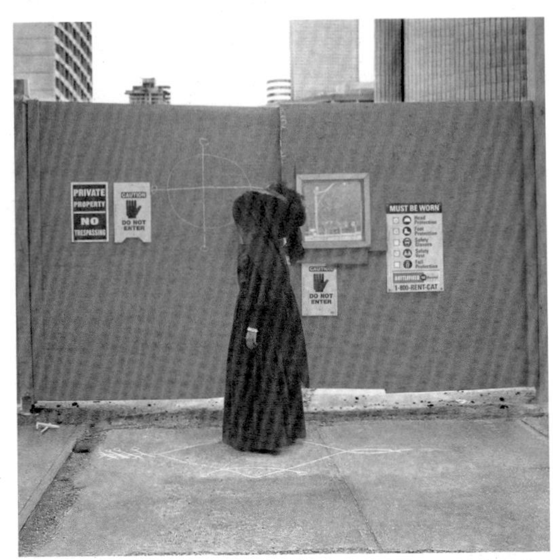

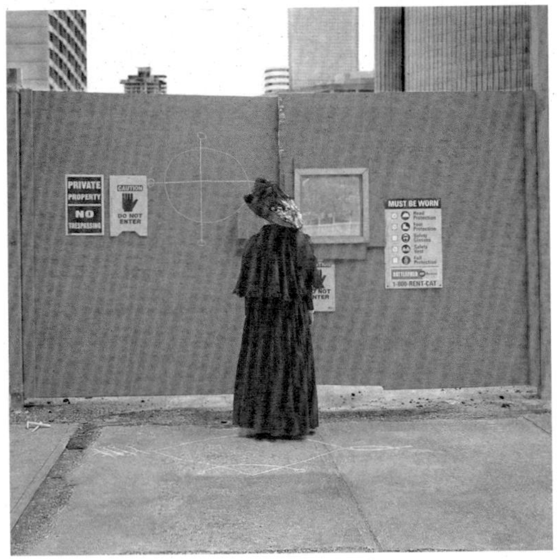

Anique Jordan, *94 Chestnut at the Crossroads* (2016)

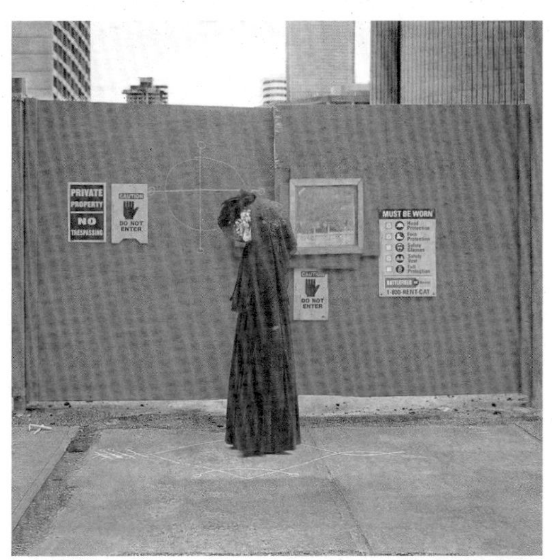
PRIVATE
PROPERTY
NO
TRESPASSING
CAUTION
DO NOT
ENTER
MUST BE WORN
Head Protection
Foot Protection
Safety Glasses
Safety Vest
Fall Protection
BATTLEFIELD
1-800-RENT-CAT
CAUTION
DO NOT
ENTER

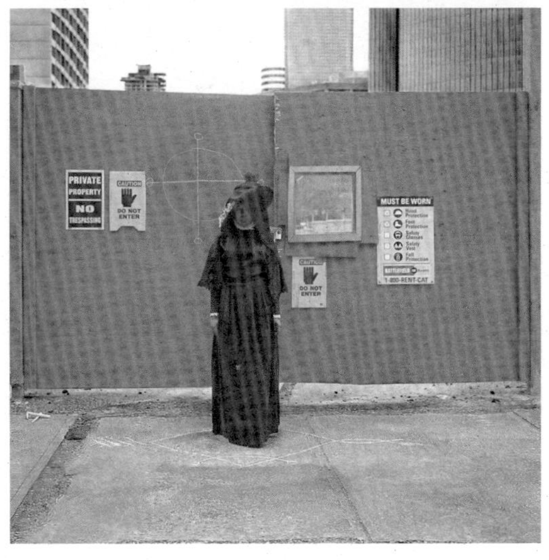
PRIVATE
PROPERTY
NO
TRESPASSING
CAUTION
DO NOT
ENTER
MUST BE WORN
Head Protection
Foot Protection
Safety Glasses
Safety Vest
Fall Protection
BATTLEFIELD
1-800-RENT-CAT
CAUTION
DO NOT
ENTER

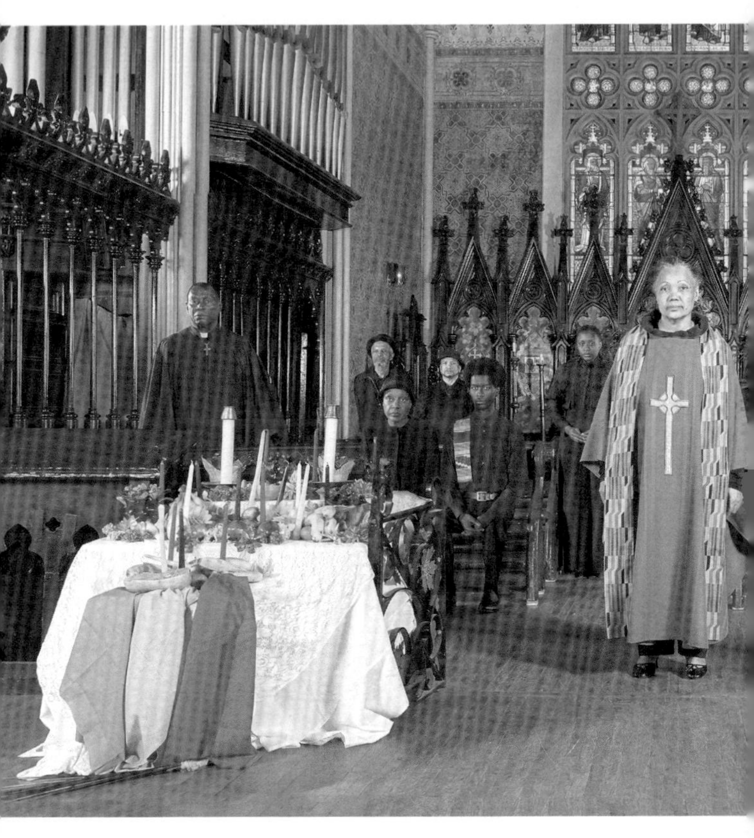

Anique Jordan, *Mas' at 94 Chestnut* (2016)

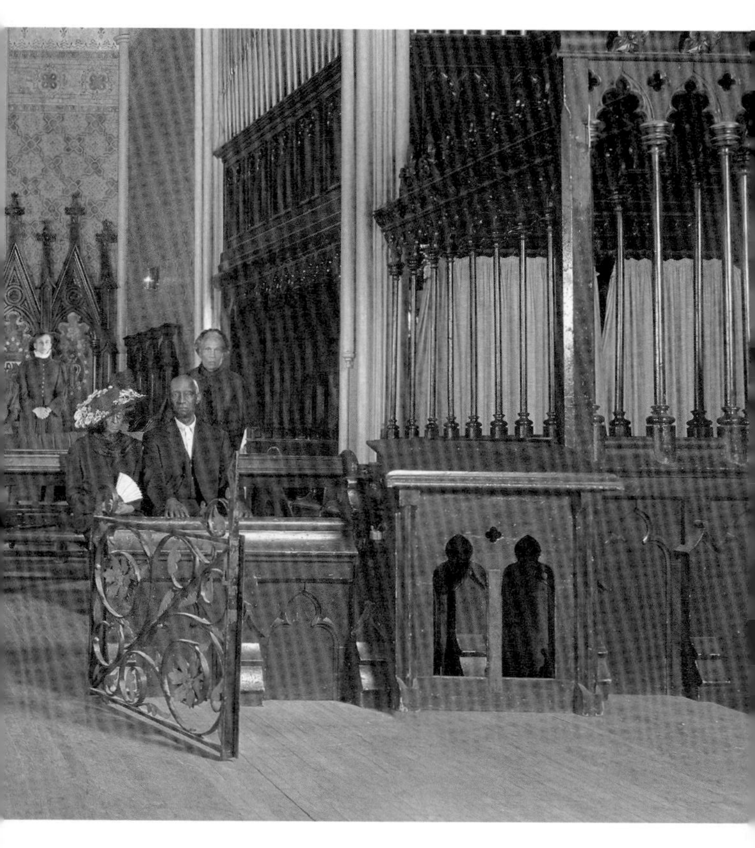

Nina Bunjevac

The Observer: The Ascent, Dundas Subway, Sunny Days (2016)

Light—as the sublime element in Harris's work—makes its first visitations in his Ward series. Dilapidated structure, solitude and poverty all become objects of awe under its benevolent influence. It was this fascination with light—in both an aesthetic and spiritual sense—coupled with dream visions that inspired Harris to leave the city and head to the most barren of northern landscapes in search of the Eye of God, or the ultimate source of life-giving light.

— NINA BUNJEVAC

In cartoonist Bunjevac's *The Observer*, contemporary workers emerging from the subway, homeless people on the Dundas station platform, and skaters in Nathan Phillips Square stand in for the three stages of the afterlife, repeating Tin Can Forest's reference to Dante's *The Divine Comedy.*

Page 134: Nina Bunjevac, *The Observer: The Ascent* (2016)
Page 135: Nina Bunjevac, *The Observer: Dundas Subway* (2016)
Pages 136-137: Nina Bunjevac, *The Observer: Sunny Days* (2016)

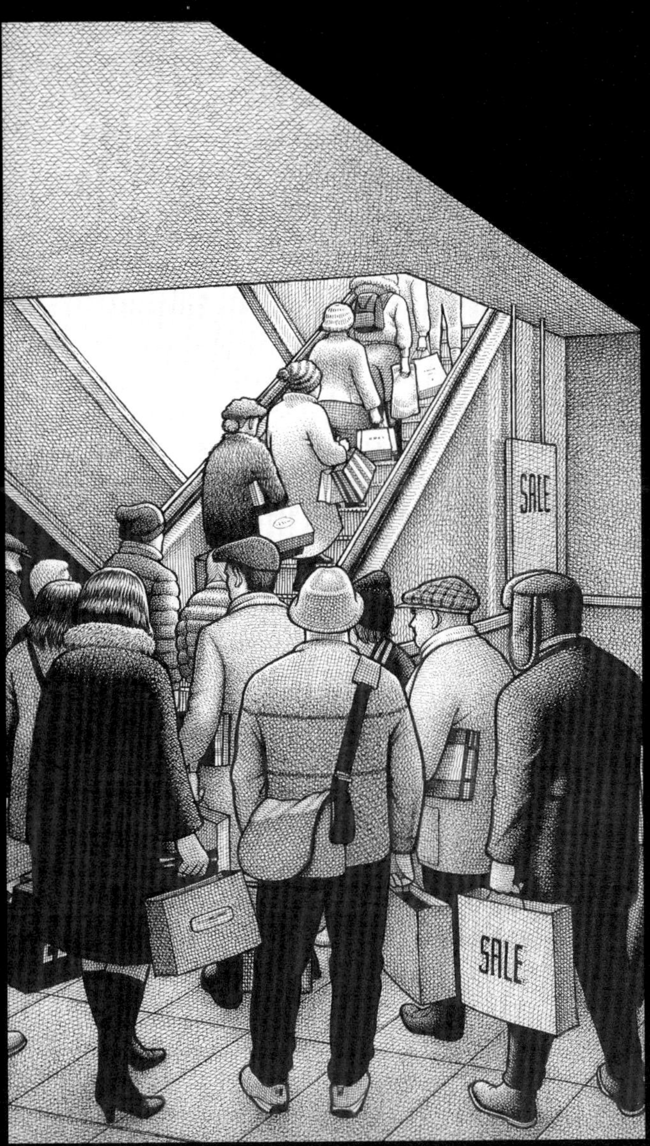
SALE
SALE

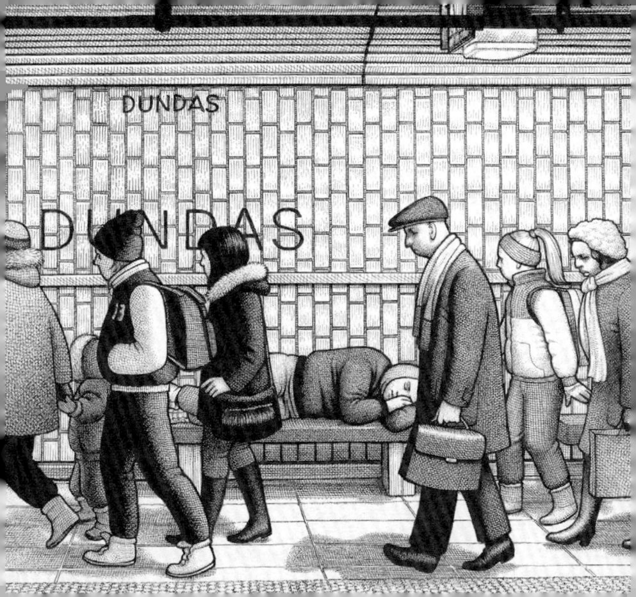
DUNDAS
DUNDAS

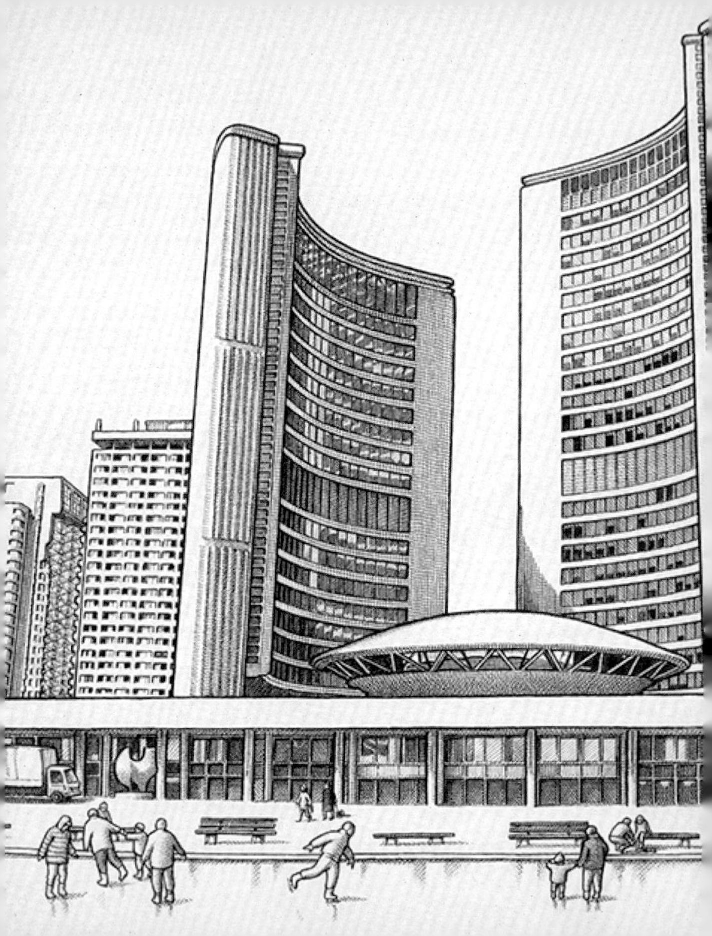

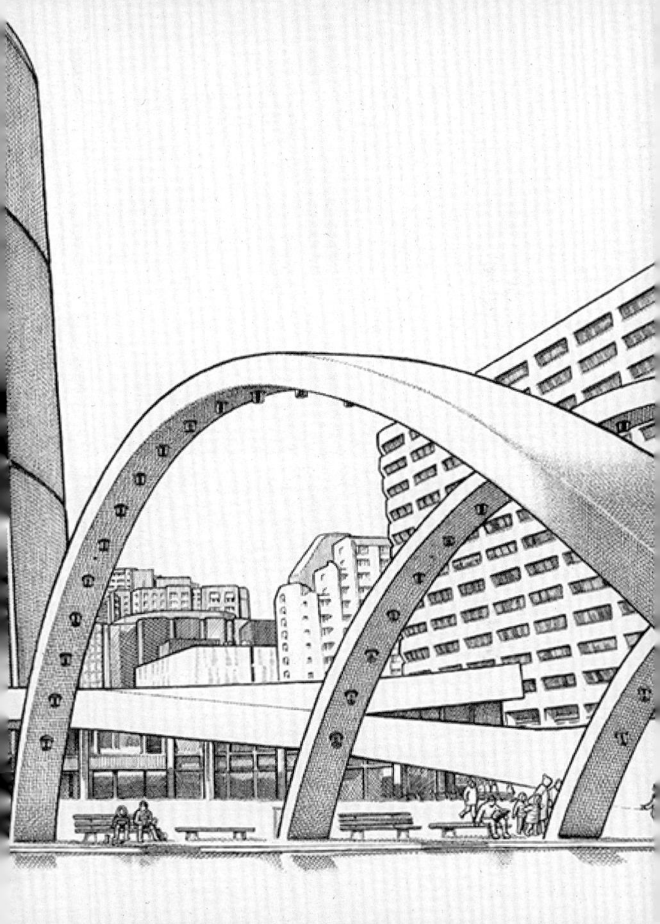

Jennifer Baichwal & Nick de Pencier (Mercury Films Inc.)

Still from video *Ice Forms at American Falls, Niagara* (2015)
Black and white still from colour original

Baichwal and de Pencier's films present environmental themes such as the impact of the human species on this planet and interpretations of wilderness. *Ice Forms at American Falls, Niagara* features a sequence of massive melting ice blocks backed by a constant flow of water and rising mist. The imagery is sublime (in its true sense of terror and beauty), and recalls the iconic landscapes of Lawren Harris. Hovering in ambiguous space and of uncertain scale, the ice forms are equally present and distant, tangible and surreal.

In this piece, we meditate on the extent to which Group of Seven interpretations of landscape inform our understanding of nature. These scenes reference Harris specifically, and reveal the tension inherent in Niagara Falls as both iconic of nature's power and completely subject to human controls of diversion.

— BAICHWAL & DE PENCIER

Pages 140-141: Jennifer Baichwal & Nick de Pencier (Mercury Films), *Ice Forms at American Falls, Niagara* (2015)

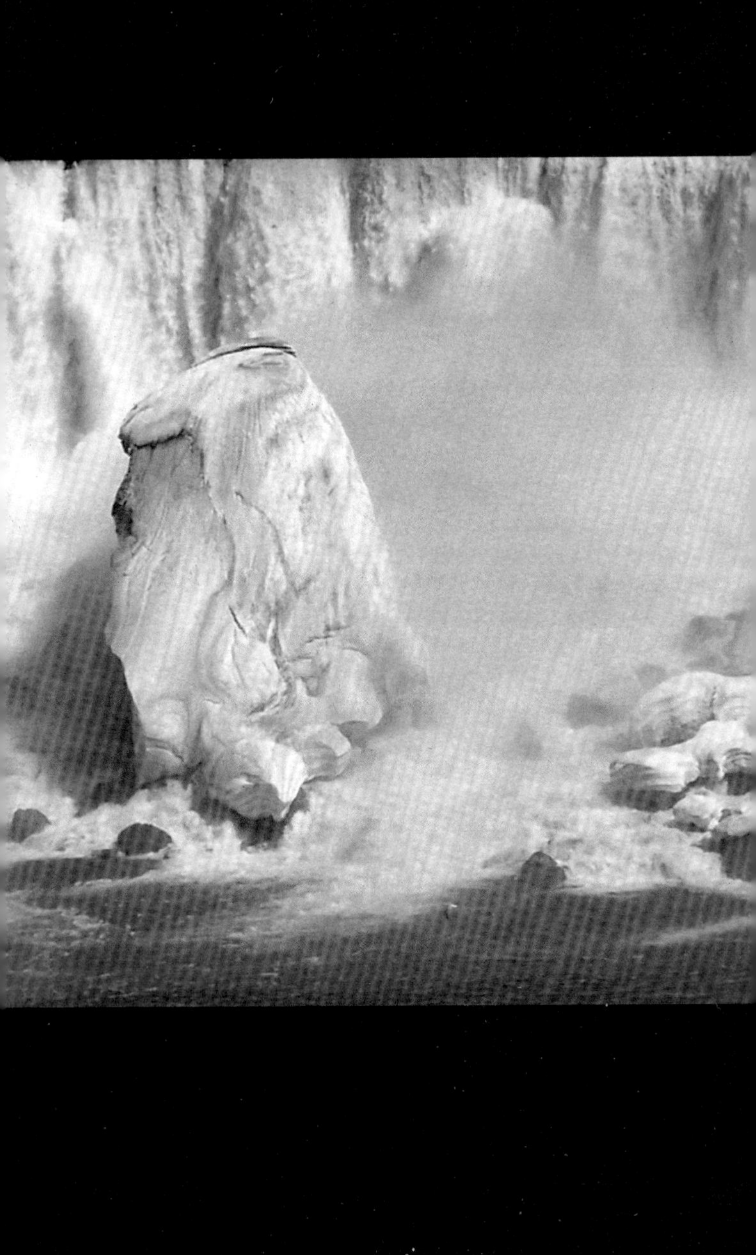

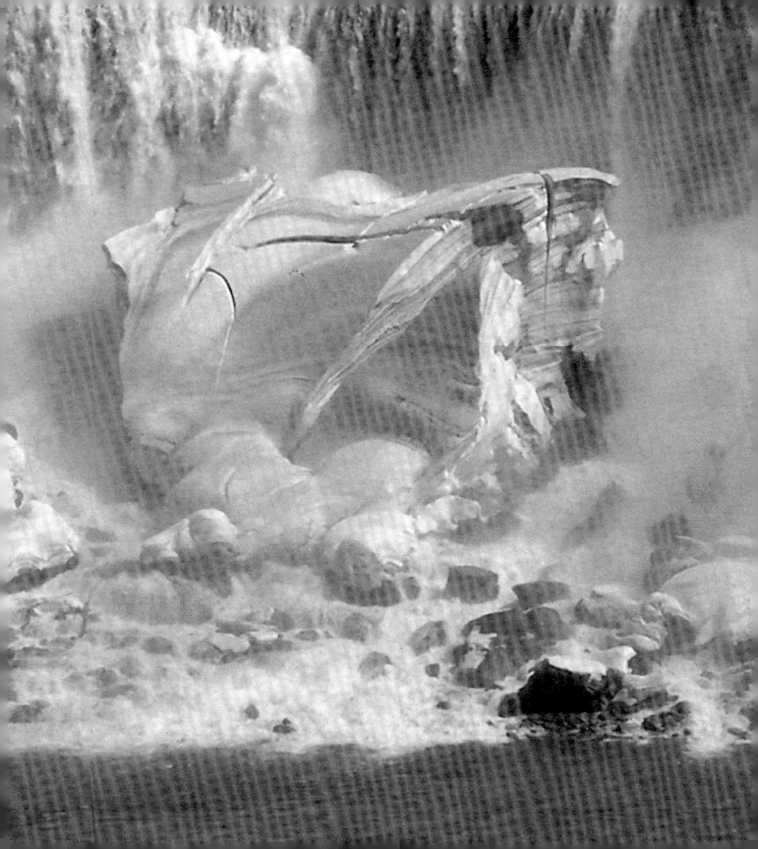

Acknowledgements

In the Ward: Lawren Harris, Toronto & the Idea of North was published on the occasion of the exhibition *The Idea of North: The Paintings of Lawren Harris* (July 1-September 18, 2016). Organized by the Art Gallery of Ontario and the Hammer Museum, Los Angeles. Curated by Steve Martin in collaboration with Cynthia Burlingham, Deputy Director of Curatorial Affairs, Hammer Museum and Andrew Hunter, Fredrik S. Eaton Curator, Canadian Art, Art Gallery of Ontario. First presented at the Hammer and then at the Museum of Fine Arts in Boston, the show includes Toronto-focused sections unique to the AGO that were curated by Andrew Hunter, in consultation with Steve Martin and Cynthia Burlingham. The AGO, Hammer Museum and DelMonico Books – Prestel published the catalogue for *The Idea of North*.

The exhibition *The Idea of North: The Paintings of Lawren Harris* was generously supported by RBC Capital Markets (Lead Sponsor), E. & G. Odette Foundation, Heffel Fine Art Auction House, The Donald R. Sobey Family Foundation and an anonymous donor. The AGO is grateful to Stew Sheppard and the Estate of Lawren S. Harris for granting permission to reproduce the artist's paintings, photographs and writings.

The publication is dedicated to the memory of Nicholas Andrew Matous (Hunter) 1995–2016.

Series editor
Jim Shedden

Production editor
Gina Badger

Copyeditor
Jeffrey Malecki

Designer
Tatjana Petkovic

Research
Samantha Benjamin
Claire Hunter
Ebony Jansen
Robyn Lew
Gillian McIntyre
Elizabeth Porco

Notes

[i] C.S Giscombe, *Into and out of Dislocation* (New York: North Point Press, 2000), 255.

[ii] Glenn Gould, *The Solitude Trilogy*: *The Idea of North* (Toronto: CBC Radio, 1967).

[iii] Lawren Harris, "Morning and Evening" (1922), in *Contrasts: In the Ward, A Book of Poetry and Paintings*, ed. Gregory Betts (Toronto: Exile Editions, 2012), 6.

[iv] The irony of a court house being built on a site of such sacred historic significance to Toronto's Black community was not lost on artist Anique Jordan, who referred to the church and the legal system as the two places Black bodies are represented—and in the case of the latter, overrepresented.

[v] Harris, "A Question" (1922), in *Contrasts,* 49.

[vi] Solomon Northrup, *Twelve Years a Slave* (Auburn, New York, Derby & Miller, 1853).

[vii] Charmaine Nelson, *Challenging "Blackface" Is Not Quebec-Bashing*, Huffington Post online, 28 May 2013.

[viii] Harris, "A Note of Colour" (1922), in *Contrasts,* 2.

[ix] Sheila Watt-Cloutier, *The Right to Be Cold: One Woman's Story of Protecting Her Culture, the Arctic and the Whole Planet* (Toronto: Penguin Random House Canada, 2015).

[x] Frederick G. Banting, "With the Arctic Patrol," *Canadian Geographic* 1, no. 1 (May 1930): 19–30.

[xi] Alootook Ipellie, "It Was Not 'Jajai-ja-jiijaaa' Anymore—But 'Amen'," in *The Journals of Knud Rasmussen: A Sense of Memory and High-Definition Inuit Storytelling* (Montreal: Isuma, 2008), 57–83.

[xii] Malaya Qaunirq Chapman, "People Hating on Tanya Tagaq's 'Fuck PETA' Polaris Speech Are Missing the Point," *Vice* online, 27 September 2014

[xiii] While Canada formally became a nation in 1867, it is widely accepted that key battles during the First World War, particularly Vimy Ridge (1917), marked the emergence of the country as an independent presence on the world stage.

[xiv] John Murray Gibbon, *Canadian Mosaic: The Making of a Northern Nation* (Toronto: McClelland & Stewart, 1938).

[xv] Tim Vesely, "Bad Time to be Poor," from the Rheostatics' album *The Blue Hysteria* (Toronto: Sire Records, 1997).

[xvi] Lawren Harris, "Morning and Evening," 6. (1922), in *Contrasts*, 6.

Image Credits

Front cover, page 24 © The Estate of Lawren S. Harris. Collection of the School of Art Gallery, University of Manitoba.

Inner cover; pages 2–3, 10, 12, 14, 16, 18, 20, 22–23, 26, 28, 30, 32–33, 34, 36, 38, 40–53, 55-59, 87 Public domain images by Charles E. Goad, Arthur Goss, William James, and unknown photographers, and from *Jack Canuck*. Courtesy City of Toronto Archives.

Page 6 © The Estate of Lawren S. Harris. Private collection.

Pages 60, 62, 64, 66, 68, 70, 72, 74, 76–80, 82–83, 88 © The Estate of Lawren S. Harris.

Page 81 Courtesy the Estate of Lawren S. Harris.

Pages 84, 90, 92, 96, 98, 104, 106–109 © Panda Associates. Courtesy City of Toronto Archives and Canadian Architectural Archives - University of Calgary.

Page 86 © The Estate of Lawren S. Harris. Collection of the Art Gallery of Ontario; gift of Hyman and Ruth Soloway, 2012. 2012/9

Page 88 © The Estate of Lawren S. Harris. McMichael Canadian Art Collection; gift of Mr. and Mrs. H. Spencer Clark.

Page 94 Courtesy the Hong Luck Kung Fu Club.

The Art Gallery of Ontario is partially funded by the Ontario Ministry of Culture. Additional operating support is received from the City of Toronto, the Department of Canadian Heritage and the Canada Council for the Arts.

Contemporary programming at the Art Gallery of Ontario is supported by

Canada Council for the Arts   Conseil des arts du Canada

Printed in Canada

10 9 8 7 6 5 4 3

Cataloguing in Publication

A catalogue record for this publication is available from Library and Archives Canada.

ISBN 978-1-894243-89-6

Inside Back Cover: Andrew Hunter, View of the Ward from BMO Tower, 100 King Street West, Toronto (2016)
Back Cover: Anique Jordan, Detail of *94 Chestnut at the Crossroads* (2016)